THE
VICTORIANS

THE VICTORIANS

INTRODUCED BY JOAN EVANS

CAMBRIDGE

AT THE UNIVERSITY PRESS

1966

PUBLISHED BY
THE SYNDICS OF THE CAMBRIDGE UNIVERSITY PRESS

Bentley House, 200 Euston Road, London, N.W.1
American Branch: 32 East 57th Street, New York, N.Y. 10022
West African Office: P.M.B. 5181, Ibadan, Nigeria

THIS ANTHOLOGY

©

CAMBRIDGE UNIVERSITY PRESS

1966

Printed in Great Britain by Jarrold & Sons Ltd, Norwich

LIBRARY OF CONGRESS CATALOGUE
CARD NUMBER: 65-16206

CONTENTS

Preface   *page* vii

QUEEN VICTORIA AND HER AGE   1

SOCIETY   47

WOMEN   103

EDUCATION   121

PEOPLE   142

THE HOME   160

TRANSPORT AND TRADE   184

BELIEF   208

Notes on the Quotations   239

List of Illustrations   249

Acknowledgements   254

PREFACE

The realm of Queen Victoria was a far-flung Empire. This short book cannot pretend to encompass it. Victorian Scotland and Victorian Ireland need volumes to themselves; Victorian Australia and Canada, Victorian India and the Victorian colonies would need others. For this reason the present volume is deliberately insular; the very few excerpts about the colonies that are included have been admitted because they illustrate an aspect of Victorian life that cannot be ignored. I have left out politics, music, the particular sciences, and, except for the illustrations and incidental mention, the Fine Arts.

I can just remember the Jubilee procession of 1897 and I put my dolls into mourning for the Queen's death in 1901. I find it impossible to be as dispassionate as I should wish about her reign. I knew only the last years of it—and those in the nursery; but I spent the subsequent decades in close relation with authentic Victorians, and for me the reign still has actuality. Old legal prohibitions, old social inhibitions, old stupidities, old failures in charity, rouse me to a stronger anger than is proper in a historian.

It is a regrettable fact that many of the Victorians who did most to shape and mobilize public opinion are either unquotable except at length, like Ruskin and Carlyle, or remarkably dull writers like F. D. Maurice and the Barnetts. We derive our picture of the Victorian age in great part from its admirable novels. Because they are still read, as much as because of any thought of their validity as historical evidence, I have hardly quoted from fiction.

The humourlessness which gave a strange, if temporary, force to some Victorian students of beauty and goodness, and the smugness of innumerable Victorian biographers, make them repulsive to the present generation. As a consequence many genuine Victorian achievements no longer receive their due meed of recognition. Euphues seems no further from us than Carlyle. I hope this book may help to break down the barriers.

Any sensible Englishman of the upper or middle class might wish that he had been born in the spring of 1834, and had died in the spring of 1914 at the age of eighty. It was the latest time when he would have had a real continuity of life, and have been warmed by a steady belief in progress; the latest when he would have enjoyed all but a minute fraction of his income; the latest when he could have left his capital vii

Preface and his possessions almost undiminished to his heirs; the earliest at which he could have enjoyed the inventions of the modern age—railways, steamships, good sanitation, anaesthetics, antiseptics, and electric light and, in his old age, telephones and motor cars. It was the latest time at which he could have been sure of ample domestic service, and have regarded war as the concern of a small professional class of soldiers.

And his wife? Ample domestic service made life easy for her; and after 1881 she had rights to personal property. Indeed it would seem best for her to have married in 1882 at the age of twenty-one and to have died at seventy-seven early in 1939. She would have had the possibility of decent education and intelligent interests. Her sons would probably have been killed or maimed in the 1914 war; but until 1914 at least she would have enjoyed the *douceur de vivre*—if in very ugly dresses—and in old age have been sure of cherishing and comfort.

And the working man? He should have been born either at the very beginning or the very end of the reign. At the very beginning he might have gone into a factory and by mere force of character and integrity have risen to be manager or even chairman; he might have started as a printer's apprentice and ended as editor of a national newspaper; he might have carried a bricklayer's hod and made a fortune. And born at the very end, he might have escaped active service in the First World War, and have profited by one of the schemes that made academic and professional life possible to its survivors. Had he gone into industry, he might be one of the tycoons of today. The latest Victorians had their opportunities; and a great many of them triumphantly took them.

The book is intended to serve as a pendant to Mr Allardyce Nicoll's *The Elizabethans* (Cambridge, 1957), though the greater length of the reign, and its nearness to our own times, have caused me to adopt certain modifications.

The excerpts I have chosen are cited chronologically within their categories. Only so can I hope to give an idea of the progression of ideas within the sixty-three years of the reign of Queen Victoria. When quoting from books that exist in many editions, it has seemed pointless to give page references.

I am grateful to Mr John Peters for help with the selection and arrangement of the illustrations, and to the staff of the Cambridge University Press for help in production problems.

J. E.

WOTTON-UNDER-EDGE

QUEEN VICTORIA AND HER AGE

1   *Queen Victoria and Prince Albert in Scotland, by Sir Edwin Landseer*

Queen Victoria reigned from June 1837 until January 1901; nearly sixty-four years as against the forty-five years of Queen Elizabeth I and the mere twelve years of Queen Anne. It was a reign of much less personal quality than Elizabeth's, for Victoria had neither the political power nor the intellectual force to achieve a Tudor dictatorship. Moreover, though the Queen was endowed with many domestic virtues, she was curiously uninspiring. In her youth she could be merry, but she was never witty or gay. Her unquestioning acceptance

1

of her position gave her on occasion a royal dignity, and her steely Hanoverian eye never lacked authority, but she could not look noble or even elegant. Even at the first Council after her accession in 1837, when she was the only woman present in a gathering of elderly and eminent politicians, her round, childish face under its black mourning cap was touching in its youth rather than more dramatically romantic; and even at her Jubilee in 1897 the tiny old woman with the diamonds in her bonnet was only impressive in contrast with the splendid concourse that surrounded her.

The Queen who looks the part usually influences the type of beauty that is in fashion; but the early Victorian painters of sylphs and naiads, and the mid-Victorian painters of St Agnes and La Belle Dame sans Merci, did not attempt to reconcile their art with the appearance of a Queen, small, dumpy, with protuberant eyes and a pursed mouth; and the increasing use of photography in portraiture made the flattery of the engravers—well-trained in providing plates for books of beauty —rather ridiculous when they portrayed their Sovereign.

The Queen is associated in the English mind with two artistic enterprises: the 1851 Exhibition and the Albert Memorial. The Exhibition was inspired, and indeed partly organized, not by the Queen but by the Prince Consort; but, perhaps for that reason, she took a great delight in it. Her *Journal* records no less than forty-four visits to it between February and October, in spite of the fatigues of a very hot summer.

The Albert Memorial, planned and erected between 1867 and 1870, is the true monument of her age and taste, both in style and in iconography. At the base groups of the four continents are at the corners, with no reference to the British Empire; America, indeed, is dominated by a classical figure with her draperies held by a baldric studded with the stars of the United States. The long friezes of artists, poets, musicians and architects (all labelled by name on the plinth or the cornice) are European, but perhaps unduly English from any oecumenical point of view. Above this base four groups representing agriculture, manufacture, commerce and architecture support the pedestal on which a statue of Prince Albert, thirteen feet high, is protected by a North Italian canopy that recalls the teaching of John Ruskin. This Memorial achieved, together with the accompanying Albert Hall, the Queen took no further active interest in the arts.

Queen Victoria had received a ladylike education; her foreign languages were good, her music and drawing adequate by the standards of her times; she could write English that was reasonably grammatical, but her intellect was quite untrained. She had no conception of science, of history, of any of the academic disciplines that were to be the most lasting glory of her reign. She could appreciate an unintellectual and sentimental Christian like Gordon, who failed abjectly as her General, and feel towards Lord Roberts—who succeeded in his profession—only affront that he moved her fan on the table before her to illustrate the tactics of a battle in the Boer War. Gladstone was prejudiced against her; but one has a certain sympathy with him when, fairly late in the reign, he looked at a picture of the young Queen in the gallery of a noble house, and said, 'She is small in person as she is in mind'.

Her subjects in Britain were fewer than we often remember. The census of 1841 gave 14,995,508 inhabitants to England, and 91,321 inhabitants to Wales. London had nearly 2 million inhabitants; only five other cities had populations over 100,000. By 1857 London was approaching $2\frac{1}{2}$ million, England had 16,734,000 inhabitants, Manchester 400,000 and Liverpool 390,600. Ireland had lost more than $1\frac{1}{2}$ million, which helps to explain the English increase.

No generation of Englishmen has been less apt to analyse their motives than the Victorians. Even the great novelists—Dickens at their head—wrote *instinctively*, with less self-criticism and less self-knowledge than would have been possible in another age. They had neither psychologists nor (except for the few Roman Catholics) spiritual directors to indicate the possibility of such self-knowledge or the principles on which to pursue it. It was the mark of the *fin de siècle*, of people who were intellectually post-Victorian, that writers became self-conscious, and indulged in the *chasse au mot juste*.

No one had as yet put a name to the subconscious, so it could be no acknowledged factor in their equations; but more than this, people exercised their authority of right, with little thought whether its exercise was unduly favourable to them. The strong and the would-be strong among them could therefore exercise power without a scruple, and law, education and economic and social conditions gave them a free field. Elders were necessarily regarded as betters. Fathers exploited the *patria potestas*, mothers their maternal authority; the husband was head of his household with absolute rights over his wife and her property; masters and mistresses had often little consideration for their servants, or teachers for their pupils; in every relation, except in a few unusually happy households, a real factor was fear. It was fear, too, that gave its force to social convention, to public opinion, and to neighbourly esteem; fear lay at the bottom of the cult of respectability. It was an age of progress, of wealth, of luxury, but it was not usually

3

a happy age for those who had others set in authority over them. The fact that some men and women in positions of power were kind, just and merciful, shows that nobility of character was not as rare in Victorian England as people of today may suppose. None the less there can be few English families that have not record or memory of tyranny to their weaker members in the course of the nineteenth century.

It was, for the first time in English history, an age of emigration on a large scale. In 1840, 90,743 people emigrated; in 1841, 118,592; in 1842, 128,592. Canada—long a British possession but still under-developed—drew largely from Scotland, as did the United States from Ireland. It was not until 1865 that convicts ceased to be sent to South Australia, though it had been granted a government and a capital in 1836. The most characteristic early Victorian colony is New Zealand. It was founded in 1838 through the enthusiasm of William Wakefield, a man of dubious reputation and persuasive tongue, who sold £100,000 worth of 'land orders' to emigrants and speculators by every device of publicity and the aid of commission agents, before he had a right to any land to meet their claims. When he reached New Zealand he found less land available than he expected, and the Maoris unwilling to sell. He acquired a good deal of their land, often unscrupulously, and in November 1840 his company was given a charter by a Parliament that knew nothing of the corruption and neglect that it was authorizing. Less than two years later, however, a Commissioner was sent out to investigate the land claims and to insist on certain reforms. The success of the colony was assured by the loss of the Maori population through European diseases and ways of life, and confirmed by the slaughter of two Maori wars. The native population, estimated at over 100,000 in 1840, had by 1870 shrunk to under 40,000.

It was a baneful effect of the fact that colonial and missionary expansion were almost contemporaneous that the Victorian Colonial Office refused to accept responsibility for schools and hospitals for other than white people in their own administration, and left such activities to the Missionary Societies. In mainly Christian possessions, such as Cyprus and Malta, even less was done. Compared with the frankly political expansion of France, the Victorian record in colonial welfare is indubitably bad.

It was unquestionably an age of violent contrast and often of conflict: between Tractarian and Evangelical; between churchman and scientist; between aesthete and athlete; between Tory and Liberal; between landowner and industrialist; between man as the dominant sex, and woman, his legal inferior; between Have and Have-not. Yet

4

in the end the balance of these forces presented a remarkably coherent society, at least in so far as it was articulate.

The Victorian age was, more than most epochs, a time of progress by trial and error. Self-congratulation was balanced by self-questioning. The immense self-satisfaction engendered by the Great Exhibition of 1851 was shaken by the military incompetence that made the Crimean War a shambles and the hospital at Scutari a horror. Any anthology of Victorian verse shows the poets of the time hag-ridden by the thought of death. The same may be true of any religious age; but the fact makes a counterpoise to the truth that the Victorians were profoundly interested in money, in success, and in *laisser-faire* economics. The age of Victoria was a time when social snobbery was rampant; yet the Victorians thoroughly understood a word that we rarely use nowadays: noble. Noble, not by birth, but by quality in thought and action; noble in unselfconscious dignity, in a balance and moderation that was neither cold nor heartless, that could suddenly be fired to inspiration.

No one then alive will forget the mourning for Queen Victoria. All England draped itself in black; white-clad Englishmen in Africa bought black-bordered handkerchiefs; little girls wore black for the first time. The regret was not for the old lady—rather stupid, very bigoted, and recently almost mindless—who had died at Osborne, but for a way of life and for an age in which a belief in human progress seemed tenable, in which scientific knowledge certainly increased, in which riches were multiplied, and in which the flag of Britain flew over lands which promised as much as El Dorado.

1

The Queen is natural, good-humoured, and cheerful, but still she is Queen, and by her must the social habits and the tone of conversation be regulated, and for this she is too young and inexperienced. She sits at a large round table, her guests around it, and Melbourne always in a chair beside her, where two mortal hours are consumed in such conversation as can be found, which appears to be, and really is, very up-hill work. This, however, is the only bad part of the whole, the rest of the day is passed without the slightest constraint, trouble, or annoyance to anybody; each person is at liberty to employ himself or herself as best pleases them, though very little is done in common, and in this respect Windsor is totally unlike any other place. There is none of 5 the sociability which makes the agreeableness of an English country house; there is no room in which the guests assemble, sit, lounge and talk as they please and when they please; there is a billiard table but in such a remote corner of the Castle that it might as well be in the town of Windsor; and there is a library well stocked with books, but hardly accessible, imperfectly warmed, and only tenanted by the librarian; it is a mere library, too, unfurnished, and offering none of the comforts and luxuries of a habitable room. There are two breakfast rooms, one for the ladies and the guests and the other for the equerries, but when the meal is over everybody disperses, and nothing but another meal reunites the company, so that, in fact, there is no society whatever, little trouble, little etiquette, but very little resource or amusement. (1838)

2

It is remarkable that wherever I have gone in my travels [in England], I have found the same complaints of the mischievous propensities of that silly, vulgar, vicious animal, called the public. Amongst the beauties of nature or of art, rocks, caves, or mountains, in ruined castles and abbeys, or ancient but still flourishing cathedrals, the same invariable love of pilfering and mutilation is to be found. Some knock off a nose or a finger, others deface a frieze or a mullion from sheer love of havoc, others chip off some unmeaning fragment as a relique or object of curiosity; but the most general taste seems to be that of carving names or initials, and some of the ancient figures are completely tattooed with these barbarous engravings....It is quite disgusting to see the venerable form of a knight templar or a mitred abbot scarred all over with the base patronymics of Jones and Tomkins, or with a whole alphabet of their initials. (1839)

3

Engaged a cook, after a long talk on religious affairs, chiefly between her and William [Gladstone]. (1840)

4

What distinguishes us from other countries is the universal publicity of our conduct, and the open avowal of our sentiments to all mankind, and I should be exceedingly sorry to find men, instead of standing forward openly and stating their opinions in the face of day, proceeding in a sneaking course, and exercising their elective franchise under a secret mode of voting. (1840)

5

I am quite scandalized at the Queen wantonly postponing the baptism of the infant Prince of Wales until the Lord knows what day in February. She seems to forget, or to be ignorant, that baptism is a solemn and sacred Sacrament and not a mere Court Pageant. A sudden convulsive fit may occur and then what will she not have to answer for? Then again as to Precedence—it is very laudable that she should be attached to her husband and show him all *due* respect. But the Prince of Wales is Heir Apparent to the Crown of these Realms— Prince Albert is utterly without any position in *the State*—therefore that he should take Precedence of the Prince of Wales is flagrantly wrong and unjustifiable.... If the Queen does not know right from wrong, those about her should set her right, for a Sovereign may not indulge in whims and caprices which would be immaterial in a subject of private station. (1841)

6

[The Leeds workmen's] beneficent principle of co-operation...was already shown in the matter of benefit societies...not fewer than 8000 working men of Leeds belonged to the Manchester Unity; but there were many other societies—Independent Odd-fellows, Gardeners, Foresters, Ancient Druids, Order of the Ark and of the Peaceful Dove, the Knights Templar, the Ancient Romans, Knights of Malta, Loyal Ancient Shepherds and Shepherdesses, and even an Order of Ancient Buffaloes! Looking at the number of members these various lodges contained, I found it was quite within the mark to calculate that the working people of Leeds alone subscribed not less than £15,000 annually for mutual assistance against sickness and accident. Ten shillings was paid weekly to a member while sick; medical attendance was also provided; £10 was allowed on the death of a member, and £5 to the widow, if the deceased brother was married. (1841) 7

During the later part of 1841...the operatives of Leeds [appointed] an Enumeration Committee, for the purpose of ascertaining the number of unemployed persons in the borough, and the extent of the distress from which they were suffering for want of employment....On several occasions I accompanied the enumerators when making their visits, and I witnessed many sad sights. Men, women and children 'clamouring' for food—willing to work, but with no work to do; not angry, not furious at the laws which kept them idle; but patient, long-suffering, and very helpless....It was ascertained by personal visitation, that out of 4752 families examined, consisting of 19,936 individuals, only 3780 persons were in work, while 16,156 were out of work; and that the average earnings per head amounted to only $11\frac{1}{4}d$. weekly for each individual....At the beginning of August 1841 wheat was quoted at 86*s.* the quarter.   (1841)

8

The man in a colony is simply a money-making creature. From morn till night, all the year round, his faculties are strained up to and concentrated upon that one object. He has no time for anything else, no time to love, no time to hate, no time to rejoice, no time to mourn. He does not seem even to heap up riches that he may enjoy them. He does not buy books, pictures, busts or laboratories, or any other means of strictly rational pleasure, for the sake of rational pleasure, but he makes money that he may *have* it, and enable his wife, perhaps, by piquant dances and stylish equipage, to excite the envy, hatred and uncharitableness of her neighbours.   (1842)

9

In no stage of literature is it felt to be so true as in the popular—that a great book is a great evil. If such a work be made public it will be deemed expedient, perhaps, that it should make its appearance by little and little. Such an age is eminently the age of tracts, pamphlets, and small books, all bearing the impress of the time, produced by it, and addressed to it. Such a literature will be more a literature of talent than of learning. It will have respect to the present more than to the past; or, should it treat of the past, it will be in works of fiction ...nor is it the least observable feature in this kind of literature, that as it asserts its independence of the [classical] critical canons...so it asserts, at its pleasure, independence of itself.   (1843)

10

It ought farther to be observed respecting [artistic] truths in general, that those are always most valuable which are most historical; that is, which tell us most about the past and future states of the object to which they belong. In a tree, for instance, it is more important to give the appearance of energy and elasticity in the limbs which is indicative of growth and life, than any particular character of leaf, or texture of bough. It is more important that we should feel that the uppermost sprays are creeping higher and higher into the sky, and be impressed with the current of life and motion which is animating every fibre, than that we should know the exact pitch of relief with which those fibres are thrown out against the sky. For the first truths tell us tales about the tree, about what it has been, and will be, while the last are characteristic of it only in its present state, and are in no way talkative about themselves. Talkative facts are always more interesting and more important than silent ones. So again the hues in a crag which mark its stratification, and how it has been washed and rounded by water, or twisted and drawn out in fire, are more important, because they tell more than the strains of the lichens which change year by year, and the accidental fissures of frost or decomposition; not but that both of these are historical, but historical in a less distinct manner, and for shorter periods.

The representation of facts...is the foundation of all art; like real foundations, it may be little thought of when a brilliant fabric is raised on it; but it must be there. And as few buildings are beautiful unless every line and column of their mass have reference to their foundation, and be suggestive of its existence and strength, so nothing can be beautiful in art which does not in all its parts suggest and guide to the foundation, even where no undecorated portion of it is visible; while the noblest edifices of art are built of such pure and fine crystal that the foundation may all be seen through them.... And thus, though we want the thoughts and feelings of the artist as well as the truth, yet they must be thoughts arising out of the knowledge of truth, and feelings arising out of the contemplation of truth. We do not want his   9 mind to be like a badly blown glass, that distorts what we see through it, but like a glass of sweet and strange colour, that gives new tones to what we see through it; and a glass of rare strength and clearness too, to let us see more than we could ourselves, and bring nature up to us and near to us. Nothing can atone for the want of truth, not the most brilliant imagination, the most playful fancy, the most pure feeling (supposing that feeling *could* be pure and false at the same time); not the most exalted conception, nor the most comprehensive grasp of intellect, can make amends for the want of truth, and that for two reasons: first, because falsehood is in itself revolting and degrading; and secondly, because nature is so immeasurably superior to all that the human mind can conceive, that every departure from her is a fall beneath her, so that there can be no such thing as an ornamental falsehood. All falsehood must be a blot as well as a sin, an injury as well as a deception. (1843)

11

A Sussex rector reports on Poor Law Administration

It is difficult to get a proper person in villages to audit accounts. My vestry clerk is a pauper, and not a good character; the two last overseers could neither read nor write....The rate rose last year 9*s*. in the £, which amounted to near £700 additional. The poor cost £1600: the population is not 800. (1843)

12

From the parish of Braughing in Essex a guardian of the poor writes, 'No cattle have been maimed, but many sheep have been stolen both in this parish and in the surrounding neighbourhood. It is not an uncommon practice to lay open sheepfolds, and to turn the flocks loose at night; to pull up and destroy young trees; to lift gates off the hinges, carry them away, throw them into ditches, or, what is still more dangerous to the public, to lay them flat upon the roads. During the whole of last winter scarcely a week passed without sheep, pigs, poultry, corn, straw, being stolen, generally with impunity. Although two men were transported for stealing forty pounds in the house of a publican, two others for sheep-stealing, and one other for breaking into a hen-roost, those punishments caused no interruption of the practice.' (1843)

2   *A portrait drawing of Queen Victoria, dated 19 August 1838*

3 *Queen Victoria's private sitting-room, Osborne House, Isle of Wight*

4   *Queen Victoria and Prince Albert: a photograph*

5　*An informal picture of Queen Victoria at Abergeldie in 1889, taken
by the Princess of Wales, later Queen Alexandra*

13

A town such as London, where a man may wander for hours without reaching the beginning of the end, without meeting the slightest hint which could lead to the inference that there is open country within reach, is a strange thing. This colossal centralization, this heaping together of $2\frac{1}{2}$ millions of human beings at one point, has multiplied the power of this $2\frac{1}{2}$ millions a hundredfold; has raised London to the commercial capital of the world, created the giant docks and assembled the thousand vessels that continually cover the Thames....

But the sacrifices which all this has cost become apparent later, after roaming the streets of the capital a day or two....After visiting the slums of the metropolis, one realizes for the first time that these Londoners have been forced to sacrifice the best qualities of their human nature, to bring to pass all the marvels of civilization which crowd their city; that a hundred powers which slumbered within them have remained inactive, have been suppressed in order that a few might be developed more fully.... (1844)

14

It is calculated in general that working-men's cottages [in Manchester] last only forty years on the average. This sounds strangely enough when one sees the beautiful, massive walls of newly built ones which seem to give promise of lasting a couple of centuries; but the fact remains that the niggardliness of the original expenditure, the neglect of all repairs, the frequent periods of emptiness, the constant change of inhabitants, and the destruction carried on by the dwellers during the final ten years—usually Irish families, who do not hesitate to use the wooden portions for fire-wood—all this, taken together, accomplishes the complete ruin of the cottages by the end of forty years.

(1844)

15

It was much easier for a youngster...to get hold of wild and violent beliefs and notions in those days than now. The state of Europe generally was far more dead and hopeless. There were no wars, certainly, and no expectations of wars. But there was a dull, beaten down, pent up feeling abroad, as if the lid were screwed down on the nations, and the thing which had been, however cruel and heavy and mean, was that which was to remain to the end.

England was better off than her neighbours, but yet in bad case. In the south and west particularly, several causes had combined to spread a very bitter feeling abroad among the agricultural poor. First among these stood the new poor law, the provisions of which were rigorously carried out in most districts. The poor had as yet felt the harshness only of the new system.

Then the land was in many places in the hands of men on their last legs, the old sporting farmers, who had begun business as young men while the great war was going on, had made money hand-over-hand for a few years out of the war prices, and had tried to go on living with greyhounds and yeomanry uniforms through the hard years which had followed. They were bad masters in every way, unthrifty, profligate, needy, and narrow-minded. The younger men who were supplanting them were introducing machinery, threshing machines and winnowing machines, to take the little bread which a poor man was still able to earn out of the mouths of his wife and children—so at least the poor thought and muttered to one another; and the mutterings broke out every now and then in the long nights of the winter months in blazing ricks and broken machines. Game preserving was on the increase. Australia and America had not yet become familiar words in every English village, and the labour market was everywhere overstocked; last, but not least, the corn laws were still in force, and the bitter and exasperating strife in which they went out was at its height.

(c. 1845: pre-1848)

16

(1) There is, perhaps, no phenomenon connected with the history of the first half of the nineteenth century, which will become a subject of more curious investigation in after ages, than the coincident development of the critical faculty, and extinction of the arts of design. Our mechanical energies, vast though they be, are not singular nor characteristic; such, and so great, have before been manifested—and it may perhaps be recorded of us with wonder rather than respect, that we pierced mountains and excavated valleys, only to emulate the activity of the gnat and the swiftness of the swallow. Our discoveries in science, however accelerated or comprehensive, are but the necessary develop-

ment of the more wonderful reachings into vacancy of past centuries; and they who struck the piles of the bridge of chaos will arrest the eyes of Futurity rather than we builders of its towers and gates—theirs the authority of light, ours but the ordering of courses to the sun and moon.

(2) But the negative character of the age is distinctive. There has not before appeared a race like that of civilized Europe at this day, thoughtfully unproductive of all art—ambitious, industrious, investigative, reflective, and incapable. Disdained by the savage, or scattered by the soldier, dishonoured by the voluptuary, or forbidden by the fanatic, the arts have not, till now, been extinguished by analysis and paralysed by protection. Our lecturers, learned in history, exhibit the descents of excellence from school to school, and clear from doubt the pedigrees of powers which they cannot re-establish, and of virtues no more to be revived; the scholar is early acquainted with every department of the impossible, and expresses in proper terms his sense of the deficiencies of Titian and the errors of Michael Angelo: the metaphysician weaves from field to field his analogies of gossamer, which shake and glitter fairly in the sun, but must be torn asunder by the first plough that passes: geometry measures out, by line and rule, the light which is to illustrate heroism, and the shadow which should veil distress; and anatomy counts muscles, and systematizes motion, in the wrestling of genius with its angel. Nor is ingenuity wanting—nor patience; apprehension was never more ready, nor execution more exact;—yet nothing is of us, or in us, accomplished—the treasures of our wealth and will are spent in vain—our cares are as clouds without water—our creations fruitless and perishable; the succeeding age will trample *sopra lor vanita che par persona*, and point wonderingly back to the strange colourless tessera in the mosaic of human mind.

(1847)

17

Howard abated the jail-fever; but it seems to me he has been the innocent cause of a far more distressing fever which rages high just now: what we may call the benevolent-platform fever. Howard is to be regarded as the unlucky fountain of that tumultuous frothy ocean-tide of benevolent sentimentality, abolition of punishment, 'all-absorbing prison discipline', and general morbid sympathy, instead of hearty hatred, for scoundrels....

(1850)

Every colony, every agent for a matter colonial, has his tragic tale to tell you of his sad experiences in the Colonial Office; what blind obstructions, fatal indolences, pedantries, stupidities, on the right and on the left, he had to do battle with; what a world-wide jungle of red tape, inhabited by doleful creatures, deaf or nearly so to human reason, he had entered on; and how he paused in amazement, almost in despair; passionately appealed now to this doleful creature, now to that, and to the dead red tape jungle, and to the living universe itself, and to the voices and to the silences.... He has returned with experiences new to him in the affairs of men. (1850)

19

Quite three-fourths of the New Zealanders [i.e. Maoris] are now missionary converts, perhaps in the proportion of one Roman Catholic to four Wesleyans and eight Churchmen.... How much, or how little, of this may be Christianity; how much, or how little, of it may arise from the circumstance of the new religion being the *fashion*, and a passport to the rich missionary countries of blankets and tobacco, it is impossible to say—nor should we care to ask. Whites as well as blacks may pray because it pays to pray; and if, by calling himself Peter and going to chapel in a beaver hat, the Maori is likely (as is the case) to become a better customer and a better man, surely his doing so is a gain to the community and no loss to himself. (1850)

20

All Europe exploded, boundless, uncontrollable, and we had the year 1848, one of the most singular, disastrous, amazing and on the whole humiliating years the European world ever saw. Not since the irruption of the Northern Barbarians has there been the like. Everywhere immeasurable democracy rose monstrous, loud, blatant, inarticulate as the voice of chaos.... Universal *democracy*, whatever one may think of it, has declared itself as an inevitable fact of the days in which we live; and he who has any chance to instruct, or lead, in his days, must begin by admitting that: new street-barricades, and new anarchies, still more scandalous if still less sanguinary, must return and again return, till governing persons everywhere know and admit that.

(1850)

We may depend on it, where there is a pauper, there is a sin; to make one pauper there go many sins. Pauperism is our social sin grown manifest; developed from the state of a spiritual ignobleness, a practical impropriety and base oblivion of duty, to an affair of the ledger. Here is not now an unheeded sin against God; here is a concrete ugly hulk of Beggary demanding that you should buy Indian meal for it.   (1850)

22

What England wants, and will require to have, or sink in nameless anarchies, is not a Reformed Parliament...but a Reformed Executive or Sovereign Body of Rulers and Administrators—some improved method, innumerable improvements in our poor blind methods, of getting hold of these. Not a better Talking Apparatus...but an infinitely better Acting Apparatus, the benefits of which would be invaluable now and henceforth.   (1850)

23

It was originally intended to adorn the faces of the ribs and stouter supports of the building [the Great Exhibition] with texts, applicable to the noble and universal purposes of the Exhibition; but the sum set apart for decorations (£2000) would not allow of this intellectual ornamentation.   (1851)

24

The glimpse of the transept [of the Great Exhibition] through the iron gates, the waving palms, flowers, statues, myriads of people filling the galleries and seats around, with the flourish of trumpets as we entered, gave us a sensation which I can never forget, and I felt much moved. ...One felt—as so many did whom I have since spoken to—filled with devotion—more so than by any service I have ever heard....God bless my dearest Albert, God bless my dearest country, which has shown itself so great today. One felt so grateful to the great God who seemed to pervade all and to bless all!   (1851)   19

6 *Silver-gilt table-centre designed by Prince Albert with representations of four of the Queen's dogs, executed by Robert Garrard, 1842*

7 *The Crystal Palace*

8   *Queen Victoria opening the Great Exhibition at the Crystal Palace,*
May 1851, by H. Selous

9 *The funeral procession of Prince Albert*

10   *The Albert Memorial in Hyde Park, designed by Sir Gilbert Scott
and completed in 1872*

Nobody who has paid any attention to the peculiar features of our present era, will doubt for a moment that we are living at a period of most wonderful transition which tends rapidly to accomplish that Great End, to which, indeed, all history points—*the realization of the unity of mankind*....

The distances which separated the different nations and parts of the globe are rapidly vanishing before the achievements of modern invention...thought is communicated with the rapidity, and even by the power, of lightning. On the other hand, *the great principle of the division of labour*, which may be called the moving power of civilization, is being extended to all branches of science, industry and art.   (1851)

26

London exhibited a wonderful degree of order, good-humoured accommodation of her crowds, and power to provide for their wants.... Enormous excursion trains daily poured their thousands [into the city]....Large numbers of work-people received holidays for the purpose...800 agricultural labourers in their peasants' attire from Surrey and Sussex, conducted by their clergy, at a cost of 2*s.* 2*d.* each person —numerous firms in the north sent their people, who must have been gratified by the sight of their own handiwork—an agricultural implement maker in Suffolk sent his people in two hired vessels, provided with sleeping berths, cooking apparatus, and every comfort...which were drawn up to a wharf in Westminster, and furnished houses to the excursionists—a foreman was there to enforce the rules.   (1851)

27

Whoever has studied the physiognomy of political meetings, cannot fail to have remarked a connexion between democratic opinions and peculiarities of costume. At a Chartist demonstration, a lecture on Socialism or a *soirée* of the Friends of Italy, there will be seen many... who get themselves up in a style more or less unusual. One gentleman on the platform divides his hair down the centre, instead of on one side; another brushes it back off the forehead, in the fashion known as 'bringing out the intellect'; a third has so long forsworn the scissors, that his locks sweep his shoulders. A considerable sprinkling of moustaches may be observed; here and there an imperial; and occasionally some courageous breaker of conventions exhibits a full-grown beard. ...Bare necks, shirt collars *à la* Byron, waistcoats cut Quaker fashion; wonderfully shaggy greatcoats, numerous oddities in form and colour, destroy the monotony usual in crowds...and when the gathering breaks up, the varieties of headgear displayed—the number of caps, and the abundance of felt hats—suffice to prove that were the world at large like-minded, the black cylinders which tyrannize over us would soon be deposed.   (1854)

28

In spite of the great heat she had on a massive bonnet of white silk with streamers behind and a tuft of marabou feather on top. Her face struck me as being amiable. Her dress was white and flounced; but she had a mantle and a sun-shade of crude green which did not seem to go with the rest of her costume. When she put her foot on the steps she lifted her skirt, which was very short (in the English fashion I was told) and I saw that she had on small slippers tied with black ribbons which were crossed round her ankles. My attention was chiefly attracted by a voluminous object which she carried on her arm; it was an enormous reticule—like those of our grandmothers—made of white satin or silk, on which was embroidered a fat poodle in gold. The Queen seemed very small to me; but of a most amiable appearance; above all, in spite of the shocking toilette, I was struck by her dignified air.
                                    (1855)

29

What the horrors of war are no one can imagine. They are not wounds, and blood, and fever, spotted and low, and dysentery, chronic and acute, and cold and heat and famine. They are intoxication, drunken brutality, demoralization and disorder on the part of the inferior; jealousies, meanness, indifference, selfish brutality on the part of the superior.   (1855)

30

Though still forced, by rule of fashion, to the producing and wearing all that is ugly, men steal out, half ashamed of themselves for doing so,   25 to the fields and mountains; and, finding among these the colour, and liberty, and variety, and power which are for ever grateful to them delight in these to an extent never before known; rejoice in all the wildest shattering of the mountain-side, as an opposition to Gower Street; gaze in a rapt manner at sunsets and sunrises, to see there blue, and gold, and purple, which glow for them no longer on knight's armour or temple porch; and gather with care out of the fields, into their blotted herbaria, the flowers which the five orders of architecture have banished from their doors and casements.   (1856)

31

November 1856. The month of November was marked by increased energy among our young men in what they denominate 'Athletic Sports'. Not only has foot-ball been borrowed from Tom Browns at Rugby by Tom Browns at Oxford, but, in addition to foot-races, hurdle-leaping, and the like, the absurd Exhibition was introduced of men (and *gentlemen*) jumping (or attempting to jump) in *sacks sewed up to the shoulders* forty yards out, and forty yards in, round a flag!

(1856)

32

You must think of me as not belonging to the present system of society, but as one looking with the greatest delight to its entire annihilation, so that ultimately not one stone of it shall be left upon another.   (1857)

33

Who can wonder at the decadence of the British constitution, when the broad-brim—adamantine institution, emblem of fixedness and constancy—betrays a perishable nature? The admission of Jews to Parliament and the downfall of the barriers of Quakerism in one year are a remarkable coincidence, and when we have to add that the same year has witnessed an eclipse of the sun and a comet of extraordinary magnitude, we begin to feel superstitious. The Quakers are about to adopt two important changes....The true, or formal Quaker Church, has not hitherto recognized the marriage of the outer Church—that is it has not allowed these marriages to be performed according to the forms of Quakerism. This distinction is now to be removed, and the true Quakers, as well as the heathen and publican Quakers, are to be married Quakerwise....The next change is on a subject of which the world at large takes cognizance—the important subject of dress. A clause in a certain disciplinary formula, which has always hitherto been imposed on members of the Society, relating to 'plainness of apparel', and which by a traditionary interpretation has always been taken to signify the regular Quaker costume, is to be removed, and the Quaker conscience is to be left free in its choice of dress. The same disciplinary clause has also imposed 'plainness of speech', and this, too, has, by traditional interpretation, been understood as enjoining the use of 'thee' and 'thou'. The removal of it, then, leaves the Quaker conscience free in the matter of conscience, as well as in that of dress. (1858)

34

It would be counted against us for a hideous blunder if after the lapse of a generation or two it were found that England had improved the breed of her horses, her cows, her sheep, her swine, her poultry, and everything animal or vegetable, but had allowed her breed of men to fall into hopeless degeneracy. But that is what is meant when we are told that the increase of England and of the whole British Isles is in their towns, and not in their villages, and that our town population is stunted in figure, impoverished in blood, enfeebled in body, and generally sunk in the scale. It is not so with those classes that can take care of themselves. In spite of several changes in our habits not favourable to health, it is believed that the gentry, and all who can live where they like, enjoy life and take care of themselves, are at least as strong, as handsome, and as healthy as the young Masters and Misses of the last century....It is not in these quarters that we fear degeneracy. It is in the working population. The population of these isles flows into the towns and there decays.

The fact is slightly compensated and largely disguised by our increasing immunity from violent and epidemic disorders, and the diminution of those diseases which cut down the healthy, the young, and the strong. A return of mortality comforts us with the assurance that the average of deaths is so many per ten thousand less than it used to be. But, whatever the truth or the worth of that statement, we seem to care little for it when we learn that increased longevity now means a longer continuance of a lower life. We may have gained in quantity, but we have lost in quality. (1858)

11 *The House of Commons, 1860, from a painting by John Phillip*

12 *Members of Parliament passing the Tellers, c. 1870*

13   *The Grand Staircase of the Foreign Office, London, designed by
Sir Gilbert Scott, c. 1865.*

14   *Bottleneck in Park Lane between Brick Street and Piccadilly, 1863*

15 *Carriages entering and leaving Hyde Park in 1872, from a drawing by Gustave Doré*

16   '*On the Dogger Bank*', *the painting by W. C. Stanfield, 1846*

17   *'The Long Engagement', by Alfred Hughes, 1859*

As slow our ship her foamy track
    Against the wind was cleaving,
Her trembling pennant still look'd back
    To that dear isle 'twas leaving,
So loath we part from all we love,
    From all the links that bind us;
So turn our hearts as on we rove,
    To those we've left behind us.

D. Maclise, R.A.   F. P. Becker

18   *The cover from Moore's 'Irish Melodies'*

From the 19th General Report of the Emigration Commissioners, just published, it appears that during the year 1858, 113,972 emigrants left the United Kingdom; of these 11,083 were married men, 13,251 married women, 36,262 single men, 22,670 single women, 8147 boys between the ages of one and 12, 7810 girls between the same ages, 3332 infants, and 11,417 not distinguished: 39,971 were English, 11,815 Scotch, 43,281 Irish, 4560 foreigners and 14,345 not distinguished: 59,716 emigrated to the United States, 474 to Central and South America, 2764 to Canada, 309 to New Brunswick, 96 to Nova Scotia and Cape Breton, 138 to Newfoundland, 316 to Prince Edward's Island, 60 to British Columbia, 21 to Vancouver's Island, 105 to Jamaica, 113 to British Guiana, 53 to Trinidad, 213 to other islands, 1065 to the East Indies, 95 to Hongkong, 78 to the Mauritius, 145 to Western Africa, St Helena, Madeira, Malta, etc.: 2512 to the Cape of Good Hope, 404 to Natal, 7214 to New South Wales, 21,666 to Victoria, 3982 to South Australia, 255 to Western Australia, 306 to Tasmania, and 5872 to New Zealand. (1859)

36

It may seem a strange principle to enunciate as the very first requirement in a hospital that it should do the sick no harm. It is quite necessary nevertheless to lay down such a principle, because the actual mortality in hospitals, especially those of large crowded cities, is very much higher than any calculation founded on the mortality of the same class of patient treated out of hospital would lead us to expect. (1859)

37

Sails and masts would probably be dispensed with, and reliance placed upon steam alone. The vessel lying low in the water, with her single tier of guns and her low sides sloping off like the roof of a house, would offer no mark to an enemy, and, indeed, would hardly be a visible object at a little distance. The change would be exactly analogous to that which took place in fortification after the discovery of gunpowder. Instead of strong towers and massive walls, the new system introduced sunken walls and low parapets of sloping turf. The principle of defence consisted in exposing no surface to attack.... The poetry of the old

37

idea will be lost. There will be an end of lofty masts, swelling sails, and graceful hulls. A ship will no longer be a splendid compound of strength and beauty, sitting the waters like a bird. She will be a terrible machine of destruction, invisible till she suddenly discloses herself, and as impregnable to all attacks as a submarine rock. The conflict of two such vessels would be like the conflict of two catamarans. A man-of-war, in short, would be reduced to the simplest form of a floating battery, moved by steam. The only object of the builder would be to cover a certain number of Armstrong guns with an impenetrable shield, to make the fabric float in water, and to propel it at the quickest possible rate. The new British cruiser would be an armed raft under an iron tortoise-shell. (1861)

38

There can be no doubt that smoking is a habit, or vice, if you please, which has of late years much increased among the upper classes of this country.... There is not a club in London which does not now possess a commodious smoking-room. But last week, the *Illustrated London News* published a striking sketch of His Royal Highness the Heir Apparent cantering cheerily across Newmarket Heath with a cigar in his mouth; His Royal Highness the Commander-in-Chief may be seen any morning smoking his way down Constitution Hill to his duties at the War Office, our Cabinet Ministers are known to smoke in their offices, our Judges to refresh themselves with a smoke as soon as they can escape from their foul and ill-ventilated courts; the smoking-rooms of the Houses of Parliament attest the prevalence of the habit among the members of our Legislature; I have myself seen the Poet Laureate enjoying his clay pipe; and I have no doubt, sir, that many of the ablest literary contributions which pass under your chastening pen are strongly impregnated with the flavour of tobacco. (1861)

39

'But, after all, it is only eleven years since the last Exhibition', we seem to hear some people say; 'and eleven years hence there will be still more to see.' When there will be another Exhibition is a question which depends upon persons and things far beyond our control; but, if time be measured by improvement or by mere change, then these eleven years have been twenty-two. Since the last Exhibition there have come up the Armstrong gun, the Enfield rifle, and iron-plated ships; several new goldfields, with a proportionate development of the colonies; the opening of China and Japan; the example of the Manchester Exhibition leading to our new Picture Gallery; the addition of Rome and Naples to the list of exhibitors; a greatly increased rivalry in glass, in porcelain, in iron, in paper, in furniture, in jewelry and many other things. Onyx marble has been discovered. Machinery has been applied to many purposes hitherto left to unassisted hand labour. Mediaeval architecture has fairly taken root in the national mind. Our ships of war are doubling their tonnage, fining their lines, and thickening their iron coats. Photography, the electric telegraph, and instruments for measuring and recording meteorological changes have made a great start. All the nations of the earth are interchanging their productions much more freely than eleven years ago. Corn, wine, and oil are more abundant, and come here in greater varieties.   (1862)

40

When any [Manchester manufacturer] boasts to me that the earnings of his workpeople average 16s. a week, man, woman, and child, I am inclined to answer so much the worse for them. It is a very great question whether such high wages are a benefit, without a corresponding high education. You must know well...that most of them do not know what to do with their money, and waste it on drink, on rich food, on finery, etc. God knows, I do not grudge it them; but the waste, and the temptation to coarse self-indulgence, is extreme....

Another great evil of your system is, that the children earn wages too nearly equal to those of their parents. Hence the family is broken up, the children are independent too early, boys and girls go off and live in lodgings of their own, and so a great deal of fearful profligacy is engendered....

Another great evil, by the masters' own account, is that mill labour effeminates the men and renders them unfit for any other sort of labour...That large bodies of men should be employed in exclusively performing, day after day, the same minute mechanical operation till their whole intellect is concentrated on it, and their fingers kept delicate for the purpose, is to me shocking.   (1863)

41

I do not think it absolutely necessary that an artist should go to Italy. There are in England quite a sufficient number of works of art to prove to him what may be done, and I think that with these and the Elgin Marbles it is not absolutely necessary that students should travel; but it is obvious that much is to be gained by travelling, the mind must be enlarged by it. (1863)

42

As soon as the summer weather sets in, the colleges are disorganized; study, even the pretence of it, is at an end. Play is thenceforward the only thought. They are playing all day or preparing for it, or refreshing themselves after their fatigues. There is a hot breakfast and lounge from 9 to 10 a.m.: this is called training. At 12 the drag which is to carry them out to the cricket ground begins its rounds, and the work of the day is over. (1868)

43

25 May 1850. The 'Cowley Enclosure' coolly and cruelly 'cut off *forty-seven foot-paths* within two miles of Oxford...substituting for them *eight new ones*'. Most of the former were connected with pleasant country-walks, and were in themselves pretty, natural and winding; the latter, of course, were dull and dusty (as being merely foot-paths by the new road side), and formal as being all in straight lines. Cowley Marsh, where at a short distance you might wander about on turf without the formality of a foot-path, was doomed to be enclosed for the chance of a meagre crop of oats on its soil of clay. Luckily the Vice-Chancellor...secured cricket-grounds for the young men, but how different (for the non-cricketers) from the unenclosed common! (1868)

44

When a Briton takes a survey of the colonies, he finds much matter for surprise in the one-sided nature of the partnership which exists between the mother and the daughter lands. No reason presents itself to him why our artisans and merchants should be taxed in aid of populations far more wealthy than our own, who have not, as we have, millions of paupers to support. We at present tax our humblest classes, we weaken our defences, we scatter our troops and fleets, and lay ourselves open to panics such as those of 1853 and 1859, in order to protect against imaginary dangers the Australian gold-digger and Canadian farmer. There is something ludicrous in the idea of taxing St Giles's for the support of Melbourne, and making Dorsetshire agricultural labourers pay the cost of defending New Zealand colonists in Maori wars. (1869)

45

The poetry of the English village names, met with throughout Tasmania, vanishes before the recollection of the circumstances under which the harsher native terms came to be supplanted. Fifty years ago, our colonists found in Tasmania a powerful and numerous though degraded native race. At this moment, three old women and a lad, who dwell on Gun-carriage Rock, in Bass's Straits, are all who remain of the aboriginal population of the island.

We live in an age of mild humanity, we are often told; but, whatever the polish of manner and of minds in the Old Country, in outlying portions of the empire there is no lack of the old savagery of our race. Battues of the natives were conducted by the military in Tasmania not more than twenty years ago, and are not unknown even now among the Queensland settlers....Where one wretched untaught native pilfers from a sheep station, on Downs, a dozen will be shot by the settlers 'as an example', and the remainder of the tribe brought back to the district to be fed and kept, until whisky, rum, and other devil's missionaries have done their work. (1869)

46

Easter Eve. Now the customary beautiful Easter Eve Idyll had fairly begun and people kept arriving from all parts with flowers to dress the graves....I found a child wandering about the tombs looking for her father's grave. She had found her grandfather's and had already dressed it with flowers. The clerk was banking up and watering the green mounds not far off and I got him to come and show the child where her father's grave lay....And then I helped the child to dress the long narrow green mound with the flowers that remained in her basket...I showed her how to arrange the flowers in the form of a cross, and she went away satisfied and happy at the result of her work. (1870) 41

It is the 21st of May, and a bright morning, and the sun shines, for once, warmly on the wall opposite, a low one, of ornamental pattern, imitative in brick of wood-work (as, if it had been of wood-work, it would, doubtless, have been painted to look like brick). Against this low decorative edifice leans a ruddy-faced English boy of seventeen or eighteen in a white blouse and brown corderoy trousers, and a domical felt hat; with the sun, as much as can get under the rim, on his face, and his hands in his pockets; listlessly watching two dogs at play....

The ornamental wall he leans against surrounds the county police-office, and the residence at the end of it, appropriately called 'Gaol Lodge'. This county gaol, police office, and a large gasometer, have been built by the good people of Abingdon to adorn the principal entrance to their town from the south. It was once quite one of the loveliest, as well as historically interesting, scenes in England. A few cottages and their gardens, sloping down to the riverside, are still left, and an arch or two of the great monastery; but the principal object, from the road, is now the gaol; and from the river, the gasometer.

(1871)

48

I have been preaching to a very large congregation in the Nave, lighted for the first time with gas. The contrast with last year was remarkable. Then, on Advent Sunday afternoon, a few ladies in the boxes, ill-lighted by candles, attended prayers without a sermon.

(1871)

49

The great May Hiring Fair at Hay, and squadrons of horse came charging and battalions of foot tramping along the dusty roads to the town, more boys and fewer girls than usual. All day long the village has been very quiet, empty, most of the village folk being away at the fair. Now at 8 p.m. the roads are thronged with people pouring home again, one party of three men riding on one horse.

(1871)

As John Cozens was mowing the lawn this morning he told me that the Foresters were going to 'walk' in Chippenham today and as this is a high day with them they were going to have a waggon bowered with green in which would be a shepherd and shepherdess with some sheep or lambs....

[The procession] presently arrived at the foot of Huntsman's Hill preceded, surrounded, followed and escorted by an immense crowd.... First came two men on horseback, riding like flour sacks and rolling heavily from side to side. They wore green coats with gold ornaments, white breeches, Hessian boots and ostrich feathers in their caps. Each bore a huge bugle and smote his horse with the edge of the sword.

After them walked gentlemen in black coats crossed with green scarves and bearing tall wands of office. Then marched thé band resplendent in a uniform of white, green and gold, followed by a waggon bowered in green branches among which was ensconced the shepherd ...in a white smock frock and broad flapping white straw hat, smoking a cigar. Opposite to the shepherd sat the shepherdess also dressed in white with a white straw hat, and the shepherd's little girl....Between them were wedged two stout sheep and a black sheepdog, and the shepherd looked as sheepish as the sheep. Behind them came another green embowered carriage with a buck's head and horns peering through the branches and Robin Hood lying down on the floor with his bow and arrows. (1872)

51

Let me ask you....Are none of you going to emigrate? If you have courage and wisdom, emigrate you will, some of you, instead of stopping here to scramble over each other's backs for the scraps, like blackbeetles in a kitchen. (1873)

52

Suppose people lived in little communities among gardens and green fields, so that you could be in the country in five minutes' walk, and had few wants, almost no furniture for instance, and no servants, and studied the (difficult) arts of enjoying life, and finding out what they really wanted: then I think one might hope civilization had really begun.   (1874)

53

I think that this blindness to beauty will draw down a kind of revenge one day: who knows? Years ago men's minds were full of art and the dignified shows of life, and they had but little time for justice and peace; and the vengeance on them was not increase of the violence they did not heed, but destruction of the art they heeded. So perhaps the gods are preparing troubles and terrors for the world...again, that it may once again become beautiful and dramatic withal; for I do not believe they will have it dull and ugly for ever.   (1874)

54

With regard to the social schemes, they seem to have made no appreciable difference. Sad and ragged figures crouch nightly in the doorways; thousands of men and women still haunt the common lodging-houses, greedy as beasts of prey for food; and crowds of weak men who might have been strong still hang about street corners and wait for a job. The fact may cause us pain, but not anxiety. The most dangerous symptom of the disease of society is not the ragged sleeper on the door-step, but the ill-paid and unemployed worker. The ragged sleeper has in one sense too much advertisement. His power of self-helpfulness has been destroyed by gifts and shelters and homes....   (1892)

55

On the whole it may be said that there has been a decrease of old-fashioned honesty, an increase of impertinence and of the habit of gambling. Under the influence of teaching, some good and some bad, stealing and lying no longer rank among the chief vices. Men and women who would not commit a vulgar theft or pick a pocket, think it little evil to cheat the railway or tramcar company, to claim as property chance findings, or to 'best' a tradesman or employer. There is much talk about what is right in little matters, but the 'robust conscience' which damns as wrong any departure from simple honesty and truth is often wanting. Mothers are no longer so stern about truth-speaking in their children...and in the schools the accepted assumption is that an excuse is an untruth. A workman's word can hardly be counted as his bond, and a promise even to join a party is not one on which to place dependence.

It is this want of honesty which makes suspicion so common in many working-class organizations, and makes it hard for leaders to lead. When it is held to be sufficient excuse for a theft that the thief was in need of bread, it becomes an easy transition to justify any action by which a poor man is benefited at the expense of a rich one.   (1894)

56

In Bristol the Poor Law expenditure is £35,000 a year...; the endowed charities are £50,000 a year, alms about £91,000, making a total of £200,000 spent in a 200,000 population....The money seems of no great use to Bristol, for there the squalid streets in proportion to the number of the poor are more than in East London, and dirt and smoke are still masters over many neighbourhoods. Unfit houses are still occupied; space and water are not within the reach of every child; and medical care is as inadequate in Bristol as in East London and begging is very common in Bristol....The result of that expenditure of £200,000 a year in charity in Bristol is demoralizing; people leave their work, they cringe, lie and degrade themselves, in order to get these gifts.... Large expenditure involves low wages, and because of the gifts men and women take a starvation wage, and therefore a large part of charitable funds goes back to the employers in their profits. One might wish that there were no charities in Bristol at all, that the poor were left to look after themselves; but that is a policy of despair....
(1894)

57

In England Sunday, as is well known, is observed as a day of rest and of public worship. Shops, places of amusement, and the city restaurants, are closed the whole day, while other restaurants are open from 1 to 3 and from 6 to 11 only. Many museums and galleries, however, are now open on Sunday [afternoon].   (1900)   45

Like 's'il vous plaît' in Paris, 'if you please' or 'please' is generally used in ordering refreshments in a café or restaurant, or in making any request. The English forms of politeness are, however, by no means so minute or ceremonious as the French. For example, the hat is raised to ladies only, and is worn in public places, such as shops, cafés, music-halls, and museums. (1900)

59

London possesses about 50 theatres and about 500 music-halls, which are visited by 325,000 people nightly, or nearly 10,000,000 yearly. (1900)

60

The cost of a visit to London depends, of course, on the habits and tastes of the traveller. If he lives at a first-class hotel, dines at the table d'hôte, drinks wine, frequents the theatre and other places of amusement, and drives about in cabs or flys instead of using the economical train or omnibus, he must be prepared to spend 30–40s. a day or upwards....The visitor will generally find it more economical to live in a *Boarding House* than a hotel. For a sum of 30–40s. per week or upwards he will receive lodging, breakfast, luncheon, dinner and tea, taking his meals and sharing the sitting-rooms with other guests....The dinner hour at the best restaurants is 4–8 p.m., after which some of them are closed. (1900)

SOCIETY

19   *From a drawing by George du Maurier, 1880*

Victorian society had a very complicated class-structure. There was, first, the aristocracy: a perfectly definable class of noble families, with the habit of governance, and territorial estates of which the tenants—whether they liked their landlords or not—had the habit of fealty. The comparatively landless peer—Tennyson or Macaulay or Beaconsfield or Roberts—was an invention of the middle and later years of Victoria's reign; and he was never really an aristocrat.

Then came a no less definable upper class: the county families of long established squirearchy; the senior officers of the Army who had bought their commissions, if of good birth; the distinguished and successful lawyers; the bankers of the great cities; the dignitaries of the Church; the more established politicians, and the diplomats, who were apt to be cadets of great families.   47

The upper middle class was more fluid. It included the richer clergy, but not the doctors except in such centres as London and the northern cities, and then only the most prosperous; the successful writers and Royal Academicians; the ship-owners; the iron-masters; the manufacturers of more than a generation's standing; the great brewers; rich men retired from the East India Company; the ordinary run of barristers (but not the solicitors); the ordinary Members of Parliament not of aristocratic birth; the country bankers; the new class of men of science; the university dons and the headmasters of the public schools. It was the men of these classes, and—with a few exceptions from the services—they alone, who belonged to the good London clubs; it was for their use that the London Library was founded and *Punch* achieved publication, in 1841. (*Punch*, however, was highly critical of their prejudices and published Hood's *Song of the Shirt* in its Christmas number for 1843.) Mudie's Lending Library, that provided novels for their ladies, was founded in 1842. Great provincial cities like Bristol and Liverpool had hierarchies of their own with special places for Quakers and Unitarians, who elsewhere could only win a place as wealthy land-owners.

Below them came the true middle class: yeoman farmers; impecunious officers; prosperous tradesmen; country brewers; attorneys; journalists; general practitioners; mill-managers; grammar school teachers and the rest. Many of them made definition easier by being Dissenting in religion or Liberal in politics.

So long as tradesmen and manufacturers lived in towns it was easy enough for them to gain admittance to the pleasant and cultivated society of professional men; but once the wish to become landed gentlemen had driven them out into the country it took nearly a generation for them to create a society of their own and quite as long for them to be accepted by 'the County'. To belong to a farming family excluded anyone, man or woman, from good society. None the less, in the eighteen-nineties a Fellow of the Royal Society could say that if you searched the pedigree of his compeers you would usually find a yeoman farmer before three generations.

And below the middle class: who shall venture to define the stratification from the respectable tenant farmers through the artisans, the innkeepers, the armies of domestic and outdoor servants, the schoolteachers, the post office, government and municipal employees, the agricultural labourers, the factory hands, the cottagers, the soldiers and sailors who were judged on their merits, down to barge-people who were respectable, and the rootless Ishmaelites like the wandering navvies and the tramps who were not? Engels, visiting England in 1843, was struck by the fact that the dregs of the working classes, people who not only lived in slums but created slums wherever they lived, were in large part immigrants from Ireland.

There is an odd contrast between Mayhew's London, in which everything and everyone was sordid and dirty except for the fine instincts of some simple men and women, and the Victorians as people of my generation and class knew them, sometimes bigoted, sometimes stupid, often ill-educated, but always well-laundered and clean.

The importance of birth and breeding extended far beyond the privileged aristocracy into the professions, manufacture and trade. The third son of a good family who became, however incongruously, a parson; the hereditary solicitor with no great sense of fact or law; the inheritor of a preparatory school, himself interested neither in education nor in little boys; the publisher in a family 'house' with no great liking for books; the manufacturer of the second or third generation with no gift for handling men or materials—these were all privileged beings with unquestioned rights. It was only in the arts that, except for a début, it was not a help to have been born to the calling.

'To know one's place' was essential; 'to be *déclassé*' disastrous. And when each man *had* his place, toadies and tuft-hunters were more easily recognizable and much more comical. The nobleman was more apt, through politics, Sessions, hunting, sport and the business of his estates, to know his neighbours of other classes, than his lady was to know their wives. The doctor or the family lawyer might be asked to dine, when his wife would not be. On the other hand the farmer's wife might come to tea, but not his son. The landlord knew his tenants; the squire's wife and daughters went 'villaging'; the parson's wife would walk at the head of the women in the Friendly Society procession; but the manufacturer's ladies were not likely to know 'the hands' except in paternal family businesses.

There was a distinction between classes even in dress. From the satin and moiré and delicate face-cloth of the fine ladies, through the middle-class merinos and poplins and silks, there was a perfectly recognizable gamut down to the prints and black serges and white aprons of the cottagers and the shawls and clogs of the northern mill-girls. Everything had its recognizable scale; the laces that went from needlepoint through Mechlin and Brussels and Honiton, through Buckinghamshire to the tatted or crocheted edge to a cottager's collar; the shawls that went from Cashmere through China and Norwich and Paisley and printed imitations down to heavy checks. Below a certain

20 *Fox-hunting: 'The Pleasures of Hope'*

21   '*The Road to Ruin—Ascot*', *by W. P. Frith*

level—a level that dropped through the reign—fashion was unimportant; but all but the very poorest wore mourning. Gentlemen still wore frock coats, and farm labourers smocks; and the grades of every trade and calling had their own proper dress, usually of cap and apron.

Carriages were no less appropriate to rank. The great houses had enormous coach-houses filled with every sort of carriage, fine if not particularly fashionable, and would turn out for county occasions with four horses and outriders. Anyone who was likely to be High Sheriff (and a great many others) had a landau and pair; then came the brougham and the victoria, with a single horse; and so through the parson's chaise and the tradesman's dogcart to the modest trap and gig of the farmer.

Even art had its social hierarchies. The aristocrats and the upper middle classes might collect Old Masters, but they gave little direct patronage to artists, except to portrait painters. Portraits by Grant and Richmond give us a vision of people who were gracious, happy, and, at all events in Richmond's Quaker portraits, enlightened; but the class of those thus portrayed was as small as the French aristocracy painted by Nattier and Drouais, and probably perpetuated on paper and canvas in no less idealized a form. (It is worth remembering how greatly the Victorians were indebted to foreign artists: Winterhalter was German, Alma Tadema Dutch, Boehm Austrian, Marochetti Italian, Whistler and Sargent American.) A no less marked class distinction is observable in literature. It was the industrialist's daughters, and their friends at the rectory, who found the mawkishness of Miss Yonge and the dogmatism of Mr Ruskin acceptable; and it was their fathers who formed a new public for Thackeray and Trollope.

Sport was not quite what it had been; Surtees had succeeded Stubbs. In its pursuit, especially in racing, men of all classes met on an equal footing. Outside the racecourse, it is broadly true that the upper classes stalked, hunted, shot and fished; that the upper middle classes hunted, shot and fished; and that the middle classes shot and fished when opportunity offered. The upper classes gambled heavily at cards; the upper middle classes played piquet and whist with great skill; the middle classes were a little apt to think of cards as the devil's picture books and to stick to cribbage and other harmless games, and the lower classes to venture their pence on dice or any other game of chance. Outside a few classic matches between great public schools, cricket and football were taken vastly less seriously than they are now; and the professional was paid and knew his place. Ladies might, after the middle of the century, play croquet, Les Graces, and even lawn tennis, but such games were not taken seriously; and it was a severe condemnation in good society of the Girls' High Schools of the last years of Victoria's reign that they played hockey. The obsolescent word 'pastimes' covers much Victorian sport.

The Victorians above the poverty line enjoyed a mediaeval abundance of servants. Every upper-middle-class family expected to employ a butler (and probably a footman) and every lady of that class expected to have her own maid to dress her, and look after her clothes. A decent cook expected a kitchenmaid, if not a scullery maid; and no good housemaid could work alone. Every household had its laundry and laundrymaid, often with girls under her. The poorest parson's wife could command the services of a cook and 'a girl', while her husband had a man to keep the garden tidy and to tend his horse. Farm servants were plentiful; and spinster ladies living on infinitesimal incomes in village houses could still afford a maid. At the other end of the social ladder, the great houses had retainers on a feudal scale with hierarchies of their own. At the end of the reign there were fifty indoor servants at Woburn Abbey, and the scale, though ducal, was not unusual.

None the less in many wealthy households there was a curious mixture of luxury in service and equipment and of austerity in hard beds, unwarmed bedrooms, cold baths and, apart from the best spare bedrooms, bleak passages.

What was good enough for servants, and it was often far from good, was in most households good enough for children. The enormous Victorian families did not encourage parental sentimentality, or luxury in nursery or schoolroom.

The abundance of servants and the general occupation of houses of a fair size encouraged an immense amount of visiting among the upper and upper-middle classes. There were innumerable cousins and family friends, and they would come for a fortnight or so (and often for months) and make part of the family. Beyond this, people called frequently on their neighbours, with or without invitation, and were easily entertained. I can remember a Victorian tea-table at which there were always eight plates of sandwiches, cakes, biscuits and so on, whether anyone had been invited or not. 'No one called' is a melancholy note that recurs—but surprisingly rarely—in the diaries of the time.

The best Victorian cooking was superb. French chefs, or men trained under them, commanded the best *matières premières* in the world and used them as artists, without regard to waste. (It took the 1914 war to make the English gentleman eat more than the breast of a partridge; 53

but what he did not eat went into the stock-pot.) In a few families—for example the Russells—an inborn asceticism restrained the chef's efforts on all but the greatest occasions. The county families varied between an excellent and intelligent *cuisine* and a puritanical liking for 'plain roast and boiled and no kickshaws'. The next class was perhaps that which best exploited a truly English *cuisine*, solid, well cooked, rich and in its unimaginative way delicious. It is often forgotten that the small farmer and artisan class had their own style of cookery—and how good it was. For dinner, first a batter pudding baked or boiled, with the gravy of the joint; then, on Sundays and feast days, the said joint with vegetables, and on some other days the bits of it boiled to rags to make a stew, and on others the gravy soup that was left, and then a boiled suet pudding; sometimes plum duff, much more often apple pudding, and then in the happy season of early summer gooseberry or black currant pudding or pie. Rather a farinaceous diet, perhaps; certainly one affected by the price of corn, but one of the most characteristic products of England.

61

It is not only absurd, it is in bad taste, for people of inadequate means to ape the manners of the great....Scarcely anything is so repulsive in a lady, so utterly plebeian, as speaking in a loud, harsh voice....In speaking to her husband, a lady may address him by his Christian name. In speaking of him to others, it is more proper to style him Mr —. To degrade him to a mere initial, to call him Mr A. or Mr B., is worse than vulgar, it is heathenish. (1837)

62

It seems to me that people are not enough aware of the monstrous state of society, absolutely without a parallel in the history of the world—with a population poor, miserable, and degraded in body and mind, as much as if they were slaves, and yet called freemen, and having a power as such of concerting and combining plans of risings, which make them ten times more dangerous than slaves; and the hopes entertained by many of the effects to be wrought by new churches and schools, while the social evils of their condition are left uncorrected,
appear to me to be utterly wild. (1839)

22 *'The entrance of the stewards and orphans at the dinner of the Indigent Orphans'*
Friends Benevolent Institution', from an etching by George Cruikshank, 1836

23   'Coffee stall, early morning', by Gustave Doré

24   'Wentworth Street, Whitechapel', by Gustave Doré, c. 1870

25 *Detail from 'Work', by Ford Madox Brown, 1863*

26   *Detail from 'Valleys thick with Corn' by R. Redgrave, 1865*

27 'Temptation: A Fruit Stall', by S. Smith, 1850

Always seek the society of those above yourself.... The man who is content to seek associates in his own grade (unless his station be very exalted) will always be in danger of retrograding. What is good company? becomes an important question. It is composed of persons of birth, rank, fashion and respectability.... If you cannot, from your station, obtain entrance to the best company, aim as near to it as your opportunities will permit. (1840)

64

They walked on together and turned down a long narrow court in the lowest part of [Oxford]. At the doors of the houses, labouring men, mostly Irish, lounged or stood about, smoking and talking to one another, or to the women who leant out of the windows. A group of half-grown lads was playing at pitch farthing at the farther end, and all over the court were scattered children of all ages, ragged and noisy little creatures....

At the sight of Grey a shout arose among the smaller boys of 'Here's the teacher!' and they crowded round him and Tom as they went up the court...into the passage of an old tumbledown cottage, on the ground floor of which were two low rooms which served as the school-rooms....

The crowd of small ragged urchins had filled the room and were swarming on to the benches and squabbling for the copy-books which were laid out on the thin desks.... Soon the smallest were draughted off into the inner room with slates and spelling books, and the biggest, some dozen in number, settled to their writing....

Every now and then mud was thrown against the window, and noises outside and in the passage threatened some interruption. At last, when the writing was finished, the copybooks cleared away, and the classbooks distributed, the door opened, and two or three big boys of fifteen or sixteen lounged in, with their hands in their pockets and their caps on.... They said they wanted to read with the rest. (*c.* 1840)

65

No man in St Ambrose College gave such breakfasts as Drysdale. Not the great heavy spreads for thirty or forty, which came once or twice a term, when everything was supplied out of the College kitchen, and you had to ask leave of the Dean before you could have it at all...but the daily morning meal, when even gentlemen commoners were limited to two hot dishes out of the kitchen....Ordinary men left the matter in the hands of scouts, and were content with the ever-recurring buttered toast and eggs, with a dish of broiled ham, or something of the sort, and marmalade and bitter ale to finish with; but Drysdale was not an ordinary man....

The staircase on which he lived was inhabited, except in the garrets, by men in the fast set, and he and three others, who had an equal aversion to solitary feeding, had established a breakfast club....Every morning the boy from the Weirs arrived with freshly caught gudgeon, and now and then an eel or trout, which the scouts on the staircase had learnt to fry delicately in oil. Fresh watercresses came in the same basket, and the College kitchen furnished a spit-cooked chicken, or grilled turkey's leg. In the season there were plovers' eggs; or, at the worst, there was a dainty omelette; and a distant baker, famed for his light rolls and high charges, sent in the bread....Then there would be a deep Yorkshire pie, or reservoir of potted game, as a *pièce de résistance*, and three or four sorts of preserves; and a large cool tankard of cider or ale-cup to finish up with; or soda-water and maraschino for a change. Tea and coffee were there indeed, but merely as a compliment to those respectable beverages, for they were rarely touched by the breakfast-eaters of no. 3 staircase. (*c.* 1840)

66

Having proclaimed that I would give soup to any persons...who would think it worth while to walk seven or eight miles in deep snow, I found today thirty-three persons assembled at the door, to whom I gave from six to eight pints each, and I purpose (D.V.) to boil forty pounds of beef into soup weekly during the winter which together with about a peck of peas, a bundle of leeks and three or four papers of groats, boiled for ten hours, will afford nourishing food for upwards of forty families. (1841)

67

Elizabeth the cook, a valuable servant, insists on wearing a collar! What must dear Ellen do? The rule of the house is that such things should not be done. She says she will wear it or leave. I say the law must not be broken and we must trust the Lord. (1843)

The clothing of the working-people [of Manchester], in the majority of cases, is in very bad condition. The material used for it is not of the best adapted. Wool and linen have almost vanished from the wardrobe of both sexes, and cotton has taken their place. Shirts are made of bleached or coloured cotton goods; the dresses of the women are chiefly of cotton print goods, and woollen petticoats are rarely to be seen on the washline. The men wear chiefly trousers of fustian or other heavy cotton goods, and jackets or coats of the same. Fustian has become the proverbial costume of the working-men, who are called 'fustian jackets' and call themselves so in contrast to the gentlemen who wear broad-cloth...characteristic for the middle class. Hats are the universal head-covering in England, even for working-men, hats of the most diverse forms, round, high, broad-brimmed, narrow-brimmed, or without brims, only the younger men in factory towns wearing caps. Anyone who does not own a hat folds himself a low, square paper cap. ...The Irish have introduced...the custom, previously unknown in England, of going barefoot. In every manufacturing town there is now to be seen a multitude of people, especially women and children, going about barefoot, and their example is gradually being adopted by the poorer English. (1844)

69

The uniform apathetic tone assumed by lofty society irks me *dreadfully*: nothing I long for half so much as to giggle heartily and to hop on one leg down the great gallery—but I dare not. (*c.* 1844)

70

We shall find...that with the possible exception of the Irish, the degree of intelligence of the various workers is in direct proportion to their relation to manufacture; and that the factory hands are most enlightened as to their own interests, the miners somewhat less so, the agricultural labourers scarcely at all. We shall find the same order again among the industrial workers, and shall see how the factory hands, eldest children of the industrial revolution, have from the beginning to the present day formed the nucleus of the Labour Movement, and how the others have joined this movement just in proportion as their handicraft has been invaded by the progress of machinery. (1845)

The men have the same tight cravats, coats too small, overbrushed whiskers, and look of being excessively washed....What is stranger than all this sameness is that the ladies look the same! The fashions have perhaps changed—in the milliners' shops. But the *Englishing* that is done to French bonnets after they are bought, or the English way in which they are worn...gives the fair occupants of the splendid carriages of London the very same look they had ten years ago.

(1845)

72

The gradual pauperization of the upper classes is distinct and tangible. I never saw so many houses to let. Barouches turned into flies, chariots into broughams. There are fewer balls and it is getting rather respectable than not to have little money to spend. (1845)

73

Representative men—men who had done something—were present by the hundred. England's greatest authors, greatest sculptors, greatest painters, greatest inventors, greatest philanthropists, greatest statesmen, greatest physicians, greatest engineers, greatest captains, jostled each other in the crowded rooms. Amid the constellation of celebrities, there were two men round whom the crowds circled, let them turn which way they would—bright particular social stars each with revolving satellites, and both receiving the deference of the great and noble as their right. One was the late Prince Consort, the other was Geo. Hudson. They looked rival monarchs each with his obsequious courtiers round him, and divided pretty equally the honours of the evening....Suddenly there was a movement, and a gentleman was seen to pass from the Prince Consort's followers and to make his way to the little court which hemmed in the Railway King....'The Prince has asked to be introduced to Mr Hudson—'.... (1846)

74

Mr Monckton Milnes put a curious question: 'Have you found the literary habits of artisans very much affected by the circumstances of good or bad trade?'

64

'Yes; but not to so large an extent as might be supposed. During a period of great depression, two or three years ago, several mechanics' institutes were formed in villages in the West Riding, because the working people had time to spare; but as soon as the mills began running full time again, the institutions were dropped. The people had simply employed in self-improvement the time that was liberated during the scarcity of employment in the mills.'   (1849)

75

Grannie was buried in the vaults of St Martin's Church, Trafalgar Square, her coffin being laid upon that of Uncle Hugh. The vaults were a very awful place—coffins piled upon one another up to the ceiling, and often in a very bad state of preservation—and the funeral was a very ghastly one, all the ladies being enveloped in huge black-hooded mantles, which covered them from head to foot like pillars of crape.   (1849)

76

Removes. These are dishes which remove the fish and soup, served up on large dishes, and placed at top and bottom of the table; great care should be evinced in cooking them, as they are the 'pièce de resistance' of the dinner. . . .

Flancs. At this part of the dinner [after the removes] there are those dishes which are called flancs, by which it is understood those dishes whose contents are not so large as the removes and not so small as the entrées, and the receipts for which may be taken from either of those departments, with this difference—instead of meat or poultry being cut up, it should be left whole. . . . It is also a great addition to the appearance of the table, and should always be served in a differently formed dish to the entrées or removes; and are only required when eighteen or twenty persons dine, and four corner dishes are used. . . .

Entrées, or Made-Dishes. Entrées are, in common terms, what are called made-dishes; of course, these are the dishes upon which, in the high class of cookery, the talent of the cook is displayed. . . . They should always be served exceedingly hot. . . .

Roasts—Second Course. These dishes consist almost always of game, which require to be sent up immediately they are taken from the fire. . . .

Soufflés. These dishes, being the last of the dinner, require the greatest care and taste in executing, as by the time they come on the table, the appetites of those around it are supposed to be quite satisfied; the eye and the palate require to be pleased, in order to sustain the enjoyments of the table; this is a period of dinner when another of the senses may be gratified by the introduction of music. . .and all ought to be of a light and inviting character.   (1849)

77

Now [my children] are old enough to eat anything wholesome (one being nine and the other ten years of age) their meals are composed thus: bread and milk for breakfast at 8, the dinner at 1, which was composed as follows throughout the week: roast mutton and apple pudding, roast beef and currant pudding, baked apples; boiled mutton with turnips, after which rice or vermicelli pudding; occasionally a little salt beef, with suet dumplings, plain and with currants in them, or pease pudding; or if unwell, a little veal- or chicken-broth, or beef-tea.

When in business, the first three years we could not afford to keep a nursery, in fact, we had no room to spare; the children then used to dine with us at 1, but at a side table with their nurse. They then had a little plain meat, cut small in their plates, with potatoes, pieces of bread, and gravy, after which, three times a week, plain rice, bread, or other plain pudding, or rhubarb or apple tart; and, at 5 o'clock, their bread and milk again, previous to going to bed.   (1849)

78

We dine alone. . .; our daily bill of fare consists of something like the following:

One Soup or Fish, generally alternate—one Remove, either Joint or Poultry—one Entrée—Two Vegetables—Pudding or Tart—a little Dessert.

This may seem a great deal for two persons; but when you remember
that we almost invariably have one or two [friends] to dine with us,

and the remains are required for the breakfast, lunch, nursery and servants' dinners, you will perceive that the dinner is the principal expense of the establishment, by which means you are enabled to display more liberality to your guests, and live in greater comfort without waste....

The following [bill of fare is] for a birthday party, which generally consists of twenty persons:

FIRST COURSE

Two Soups—Two Fish

Removes. Haunch of Mutton—Broiled Capons à l'Ecarlate.
Flancs. Fricandeau of Veal—Currie of Fowl.
Entrées. Fillets of Beef, sauce Tomate—Cutlets Soubise—Oyster Patties, or Little Vol-au-Vent; Croquettes of Veal or Fowl.

SECOND COURSE

Wild Ducks—Guinea Fowl larded—Charlotte Russe—Punch Jelly—Crusts of Fruit—Flanc Meringue—Apple with Rice—Scolloped Oysters—Mayonnaise of Fowl—Sea Kale or Asparagus.
Removes. Turban of Condé Glacée—Cheese Soufflé à la Vanille.
Dessert of nineteen dishes.

(1849)

79

Dinner was served pretty punctually, only half an hour after time. On my entrance in the room my first glance at the table showed me that there was a want of *savoir-faire* in its management; the plate, very abundant and splendid, was of so yellow a cast that it looked as if it were plated, and the cut glass was exceedingly dim. My first surprise was that there were no napkins, the next the soup plates were quite cold...; after being served with fish, and waiting until it was cold for the sauce to eat with it, I was rather sceptical how the rest of the dinner would progress. After the first, the second course made its appearance, which was heavy and too abundant; the plain things were well done, but there was only one servant in the room for the whole party of fourteen, and from the strict formality of the table, it would have been a sacrilege to have handed your plate for any vegetables, or anything else you might require. There were four saltcellars, certainly

Society   very massive silver ones, at each corner of the table, and a beautiful cruet-frame in the centre; the hot dishes of this course, like the previous one, became cold and tasteless before being eaten, and during the time the servant was serving the champagne all the plates were empty; in fact it was a good dinner spoilt....

About half an hour after the cloth was removed, and just as the conversation was being thawed from the freezing it received at the dinner table, Mrs D. and the ladies withdrew, and for an hour and a half we had to bear the insipid conversation of the drawing-room, the hissing urn at the tea-table bearing a prominent part. Several messages were sent from time to time to the dining-room to say that coffee was ready; and when at last the gentlemen came, two had had quite wine enough, which caused them to receive sundry angry looks from their wives who were present....   (1849)

28   '*Going to Table*', *from a drawing by George du Maurier*

I inclose the bill of fare of a dinner given by — Bass, Esq., M.P., at the Reform Club, the other day....

Reform Club
7 juillet 1849

Diner pour 18 personnes

Deux Potages
One Thick Turtle
One Clear Ditto
Deux Poissons
Crimped Salmon en Matelote Normande
Turbot à la Richelieu
Deux Relevés
La Hanche de Venaison aux haricots verts
Les Poulardes en Diadème
Six Entrées

Vol-au-Vent de Foie Gras à la Talleyrand
Côtelettes d'Agneau demi Provençale
Petits Canetons Canaris aux jeunes légumes glacées
Noix de Veau demi grasse à la purée de Concombres
Ortolans à la Vicomtesse
Aiguillettes de petits Poussins à la Banquière
Deux Rôtis
Les *Turkey Poults* piqués et bardés, garnis de Cailles
aux feuilles de vignes
Les jeunes Levrauts au jus de groseilles
[Small side dishes]
Rissollettes à la Pompadour
Petites Croquants aux œufs de Rougets
Huits Entremets

Gelée à l'eau de vie de Dantzick
Aspic de Homard à la Gelée
Petits Pois à l'anglaise
Pain de Pêches au noyau

Flanc d'Abricôts aux Liqueurs
Quartiers d'artichaux à la
Venétienne
Gateau Milanais au Parmesan
Bombe glacée au Café Moka

Jambon en surprise glacé à la Vanille
Pudding à la Méphistophiles

29 'The children of Elhanan Bicknell', by S. P. Denning, 1841

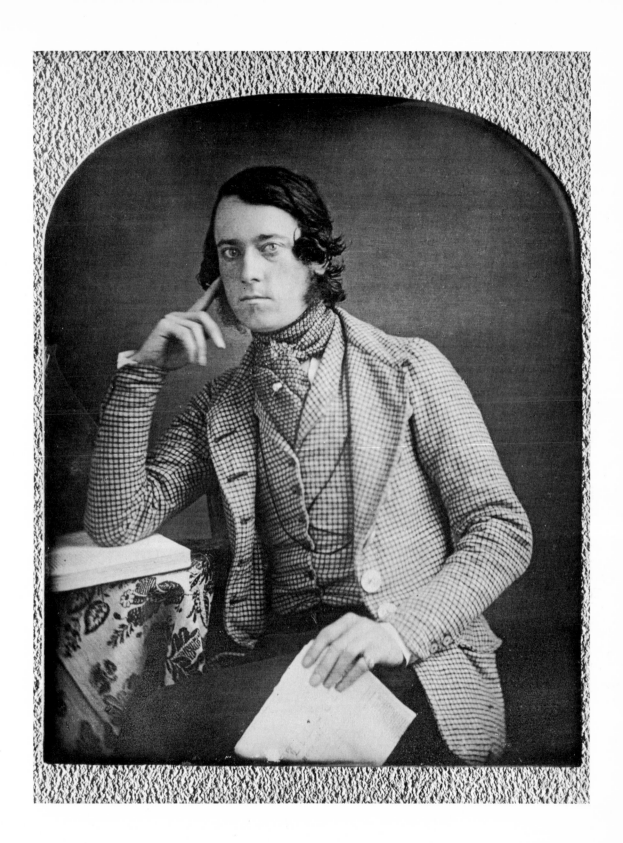

30 *Daguerreotype of a gentleman, c. 1845*

31 'Ramsgate Sands', by W. P. Frith

32   'Bedtime', by Arthur Hughes

Several months ago, some friends took me with them to see one of the London Prisons, a prison of the exemplary or model kind. An immense circuit of buildings; cut out first with a high ring-wall, from the lanes and streets of the quarter, which is a dim and crowded one. Gateway as to a fortified place; then a spacious court, like the square of a city; broad staircases, passages to inferior courts; fronts of stately architecture all round....Surely one of the most perfect buildings within the compass of London...probably no Duke in England lives in a mansion of such perfect and thorough cleanliness....Hopeless for ever now [the project of governing prisoners by 'the method of love']. These abject, ape, wolf, ox, imp and other diabolic animal specimens of humanity, who of the very gods could ever have commanded them by love? A collar round the neck, and a cartwhip flourished over the back; these in a just and steady human hand, were what the gods would have appointed them....   (1850)

82

Many things have been written about shirt-making; but here perhaps is the saddest of all, not written anywhere till now, that I know of. Shirts by the thirty-thousand are made at $2\frac{1}{2}d.$ each;—and in the meanwhile no needle-woman, distressed or other, can be procured in London by any housewife to give for fair wages, fair help in sewing...good sempstresses are to be hired in every village; in London, with its famishing 30,000, not at all, or hardly.   (1850)

83

It is almost a definition of a gentleman to say he is one who never inflicts pain....He is mainly occupied in merely removing the obstacles which hinder the free and unembarrassed action of those about him; and he concurs with their movements rather than takes the initiative himself....The true gentleman...carefully avoids whatever may cause a jar or a jolt in the minds of those with whom he is cast—all clashing of opinion, or collision of feeling, all restraint, or suspicion, or gloom or resentment; his great concern being to make everyone at   75 their ease and at home...he makes light of favours while he does them, and seems to be receiving when he is conferring. He never speaks of himself except when compelled, never defends himself by a mere retort, he has no ears for slander or gossip, is scrupulous in imputing motives to those who interfere with him, and interprets everything for the best....If he engages in controversy of any kind, his disciplined intellect preserves him from the blundering discourtesy of better, perhaps, but less educated minds....He may be right or wrong in his opinion, but he is too clear-headed to be unjust; he is as simple as he is forcible, and as brief as he is decisive....If he be an unbeliever, he will be too profound and large-minded to ridicule religion or to act against it; he is too wise to be a dogmatist or fanatic in his infidelity. He respects piety and devotion; he even supports institutions as venerable, beautiful, or useful, to which he does not assent....He is a friend of religious toleration and that, not only because his philosophy has taught him to look on all forms of faith with an impartial eye, but also from the gentleness and effeminacy of feeling, which is the attendant of civilization. (1852)

84

We have much studied and much perfected, of late, the great civilized invention of the division of labour; only we give it a false name. It is not, truly speaking, the labour that is divided, but the men; divided into mere segments of men—broken into small fragments and crumbs of life; so that all the little piece of intelligence that is left in a man is not enough to make a pin or a nail, but exhausts itself in making the point of a pin or the head of a nail. Now it is a good and desirable thing, truly, to make many pins in a day; but if we could only see with what crystal sand their points were polished—sand of human soul, much to be magnified before it can be discerned for what it is—we should think there might be some loss in it also. And the great cry that rises from all our manufacturing cities, louder than their furnace blast, is all in very deed for this, that we manufacture everything there except men....It can be met only by a right understanding, on the part of all classes, of what kinds of labour are good for men, raising them, and making them happy; by a determined sacrifice of such convenience, or beauty, or cheapness as is to be got only by the degradation of the workman; and by equally determined demand for the

products and results of healthy and ennobling labour.

And how, it will be asked, are these products to be recognized, and $Society$
this demand to be regulated? Easily: by the observance of three
broad and simple rules:

(1) Never encourage the manufacture of any article not absolutely
necessary, in the production of which *invention* has no share.

(2) Never demand an exact finish for its own sake, but only for some
practical or noble end.

(3) Never encourage imitation or copying of any kind, except for the
sake of preserving record of great works.

The second of these principles is the only one which directly rises out
of the consideration of our immediate subject; but I shall briefly explain the meaning and extent of the first also, reserving the enforce-
ment of the third for another place.

(1) *Never encourage the manufacture of anything not necessary, in the
production of which invention has no share.*

For instance. Glass beads are utterly unnecessary, and there is no
design or thought employed in their manufacture. They are formed by
first drawing out the glass into rods; these rods are chopped up into
fragments of the size of beads by the human hand, and the fragments
are then rounded in the furnace. The men who chop up the rods sit at
their work all day, their hands vibrating with a perpetual and exquisitely timed palsy, and the beads dropping beneath their vibration
like hail. Neither they, nor the men who draw out the rods or fuse the
fragments, have the smallest occasion for the use of any single human
faculty; and every young lady, therefore, who buys glass beads is engaged in the slave-trade, and in a much more cruel one than that which
we have so long been endeavouring to put down.

But glass cups and vessels may become the subjects of exquisite invention; and if in buying these we pay for the invention, that is to say
for the beautiful form, or colour, or engraving, and not for mere finish
of execution, we are doing good to humanity.

I shall only give one example, which however will show the reader
what I mean, from the manufacture already alluded to, that of glass.
Our modern glass is exquisitely clear in its substance, true in its form,
accurate in its cutting. We are proud of this. We ought to be ashamed
of it. The old Venice glass was muddy, inaccurate in all its forms, and
clumsily cut, if at all. And the old Venetian was justly proud of it.
For there is this difference between the English and Venetian workman, that the former thinks only of accurately matching his patterns,
and getting his curves perfectly true and his edges perfectly sharp, and
becomes a mere machine for rounding curves and sharpening edges, 77

while the old Venetian cared not a whit whether his edges were sharp or not, but he invented a new design for every glass that he made, and never moulded a handle or a lip without a new fancy in it. And therefore, though some Venetian glass is ugly and clumsy enough, when made by clumsy and uninventive workmen, other Venetian glass is so lovely in its forms that no price is too great for it; and we never see the same form in it twice. Now you cannot have the finish and the varied form too. If the workman is thinking about his edges, he cannot be thinking of his design; if of his design, he cannot think of his edges. Choose whether you will pay for the lovely form or the perfect finish, and choose at the same moment whether you will make the worker a man or a grindstone. (1853)

85

...A day of national humiliation was appointed on the outbreak of the Crimean War. Severely indeed was the fast-day observed at Hurstmonceaux....We had nothing to eat but bread, and for dinner some boiled sea-kale....I have a vivid remembrance of the serio-comic face of our butler...when we were ushered into the dining-room with the table laid out as usual, and, when the covers were taken off, only that amount of food was displayed. (1854)

86

He thought it very desirable to connect the higher classes of Society with the Army; and he did not know any more effective method of connecting them than by allowing members of high families who held commissions to get on with more rapidity than they would by seniority [by purchase]. If the connexion between the Army and the higher class of society were dissolved, then the Army would present a dangerous and unconstitutional appearance. It was only when the Army was unconnected with those whose property gave them an interest in the Country, and was commanded by unprincipled military adventurers, that it ever became formidable to the liberties of the

nation. (1856)

Q. What are the classes of society?

A. Proprietors, money-dealers, farmers, manufacturers, traders, professions, servants, and labourers....

Q. What are money-dealers?

A. Persons who live on the interest of money, by lending it on some security.   (1856)

88

Q. What are honest practices?

A. Respect to the property and just rights of others, and living on our own means and industry.   (1856)

89

English Dinners
To the Editor of *The Times*

If I have understood your comments...rightly, sir, you wish the middle classes to dine well at a moderate expense, to show their appreciation of their guests by catering for their real tastes and private predilections, instead of slavishly subjecting themselves and friends to mere fashion.... Reduce the number of dishes of all kinds, whether head, side, or corner; vary the kind for your guests as you would for your self, and try and exercise such an amount of taste in the selection and succession of the viands as, without hoping to arrive at the glories of Berkeley-square, may gratify your guests as well by the novelty as by the implied compliment to their gustatory education.

I cannot better...illustrate my meaning than by quoting the opinion of the clever *Memoirs of a Stomach*, who, equally with yourself, deprecates unnecessary dishes. The author is a dyspeptic—what regular diner-out is not?—and declares soup as a foundation for dinner to be simply an abomination; and so it is (*credat dyspepticus*). He then enunciates the following brief apothegm; viz. 'a nice small turbot with lobster sauce, a neck of doe-venison in season, with a couple of woodcocks, is a dinner for an emperor'. Add, say I, a couple of young chickens (not rabbits) with a jelly and one *mange*—red, white, or blue, for the ladies—and there's your dinner for

Yours etc.

One who Feels he has a Stomach

Worcester, Jan. 15

November, 1859. In chronicling the striking incidents and varying shades of Oxford life, it is but fair to mention the following notice, by the Vice-Chancellor and Proctors, as a proof of a growing neglect of manners, the natural accompaniment of a rougher bearing and a coarser *external*: 'Whereas complaints have been made that some undergraduate members of the University are in the habit of smoking at *public entertainments* and otherwise creating annoyance, they are hereby cautioned against the repetition of such ungentlemanlike conduct.'   (1859)

91

Had a dinner-party on the sensible principle enunciated by some letter-writers to *The Times* and called *à la Russe*. It consists in having fruit and flowers on the table, with wine, etc., the abolition of side-dishes, and only one dish at a time placed opposite the host. The plan worked very well, and the cook said that it was much easier for her.   (1859)

92

During the summer months and fruit season, the average number of costermongers attending Covent Garden market is about 2500 per market day. In the strawberry season there are nearly double as many....

I am informed...that there are 18,000 itinerant and stationary street sellers of fish, vegetables and fruit in the metropolis; and reckoning the same proportion of wives and children (to help them) as before, we have thus 45,000 men, women and children obtaining a living in this manner....

But great as is this number, still the costermongers are only a portion of the street-folk....The street musicians, for instance, are said to number 1000 and the old clothes-men the same. There are supposed to be at the least 500 sellers of water-cresses; 200 coffee stalls; 300 Cats' meat men; 250 ballad-singers; 200 play-bill sellers; from 800 to 1000 bone-grubbers and mudlarks; 1000 crossing-sweepers; another thousand chimney sweeps, and the same number of turncocks and lamplighters all of whom, together with the street-performers and showmen,

turnkeys, chair, umbrella and clock-menders, sellers of bonnet-boxes, Society
toys, stationery, songs, last dying-speeches, tubs, pails, mats, crockery,
blacking, lucifers, corn-salves, clothes-pegs, brooms, sweetmeats,
razors, dog-collars, dogs, birds, coals, seed,—scavengers, dustmen
and others, make up, it may be fairly assumed, full 30,000 adults, so
that reckoning men, women and children, we may truly say that there
are upwards of 50,000 individuals, or about a fortieth part of the entire population of the metropolis, getting their living in the streets.

Now of all modes of obtaining subsistence, that of street-selling is the
most precarious. Continued wet weather deprives those who depend
for their bread upon the number of people frequenting the public
thoroughfares of all means of living; and it is painful to think of the
hundreds belonging to this class in the metropolis who are reduced to
starvation by three or four days' successive rain. (1861)

93

On a good attractive night, the rush of costers to the 3*d.* gallery of the
Coburg (better known as 'the Vic') is peculiar and almost awful.

The long zig-zag staircase that leads to the pay-box is crowded to
suffocation at least an hour before the theatre is opened; but, on the
occasion of a piece with a good murder in it, the crowd will frequently
collect as early as 3 o'clock in the afternoon.

There are few grown-up men that go to the 'Vic' gallery. The gen-
erality of the visitors are lads from about twelve to three-and-twenty,
and though a few black-faced sweeps or whitey-brown dustmen may
be among the throng, the gallery audience consists mainly of costermongers. Young girls, too, are very plentiful, only one-third of whom
now take their babies, owing to the new regulation of charging half-
price for infants....

It is the fashion with the mob to take off their coats, and the cross-
braces on the backs of some, and the bare shoulders peeping out of the
ragged shirts of others, are the only variety to be found. The bonnets
of the 'ladies' are hung over the iron railing in front, their numbers
nearly hiding the panels, and one of the amusements of the lads in the
back seats consists in pitching orange peel or nutshells into them, a
good aim being rewarded with a shout of laughter.

When the orchestra begins playing, before 'the gods' have settled
into their seats, it is impossible to hear a note of music. The puffed-out
cheeks of the trumpeters, and the raised drumsticks, tell you that the 81

overture has commenced, but no tune is to be heard, an occasional burst of the full band being caught by gushes, as if a high wind were raging.... Presently a fight is sure to begin, and then everyone rises from his seat whistling and shouting; three or four pairs of arms fall to, the audience waving their hands till the moving mass seems like microscopic eels in paste. But the commotion ceases suddenly at the rising of the curtain....

The 'Vic' gallery is not to be moved by touching sentiment. They prefer vigorous exercise to any emotional speech.... The dances and comic songs, between the pieces, are liked better than anything else. A highland fling is certain to be repeated, and a stamping of feet will accompany the tune, and a shrill whistling keep time through the entire performance.

But the grand hit of the evening is always when a song is sung in which the entire gallery can join in chorus. Then a deep silence prevails through all the stanzas. Should any burst in before his time a shout of 'orda-a-r' is raised, and the intruder put down by a thousand indignant cries. At the proper time, however, the throats of the mob burst forth in all their strength. The most deafening noise breaks out suddenly, while the catcalls keep up the tune, and an imitation of a dozen Mr Punches squeak out the words.... (1861)

94

A well-to-do 'coster', when dressed for the day's work, usually wears a small cloth cap, a little on one side. A close-fitting worsted tie-up skull-cap is very fashionable just now among the class, and ringlets at the temples are looked up to as the height of elegance. Hats they never wear—excepting on Sunday—on account of their baskets being frequently carried on their heads. Coats are seldom indulged in; their waistcoats, which are of a broad-ribbed corduroy, with fustian back and sleeves, being made as long as a groom's, and buttoned up nearly to the throat. If the corduroy be of a light sandy colour, then plain brass, or sporting buttons, with raised fox's or stag's heads upon them —or else blackbone-buttons with a flower pattern—ornament the front; but if the cord be of a dark ratskin hue, then mother-of-pearl buttons are preferred.... The fashionable stuff for trousers, at the present, is a dark-coloured 'cable cord', and they are made to fit tightly at the knee

and swell gradually until they reach the boot, which they nearly cover.

... The man who does not wear his silk neckerchief—his 'King's man' as it is called—is known to be in desperate circumstances; the inference being that it has gone to supply the morning's stock-money. A yellow flower on a green ground, or a red and blue pattern, is at present greatly in vogue. The women wear their kerchiefs tucked-in under their gowns, and the men have theirs wrapped loosely round the neck, with the ends hanging over their waistcoats. Even if a costermonger has two or three silk handkerchiefs by him already he seldom hesitates to buy another, when tempted with a bright showy pattern hanging from a Field-lane doorpost.

(1861)

95

My neighbourhood contains a purely agricultural population, the heads of which are proprietors on a moderate scale, and tenant farmers, none of them wealthy. The farms and cottages lie for the most part scattered along hill and dale, on a rich moist soil, which causes great wear and tear of clothes, especially shoe leather. Stone is plentiful, which occasions good dwellings at reasonable rents, excepting where you are near a town. But ways are difficult and conveniences few, which all tends to expense.

You may put the farm labourer's wages at from 8s. to 10s. a week and his cider. The *maximum* is reached only by the carter and head shepherd, and then it is usually paid thus—8s. per week, with a cottage, small garden and twenty perches of potato ground, and an allowance of firewood. These allowances are valued at 2s. per week....

A carter's and shepherd's wages never vary, but a good labourer has the chance of piecework, by which, if he is skilful, he will earn more than his day's wages. Reaping, mowing, hoeing, wooding, are all done by measure. A man on piecework will hardly cease his labour while the light serves him, even in summer. This is his only chance of getting a little beforehand with the world. Cottages may be had of the largest proprietors for from 1s. to 1s. 6d. a week, but the small landlord invariably asks, and gets, more. Coals may be put at 1s. per cwt.

The rate at which boys are paid is in small proportion to the men; 6d. a week is gladly taken by a poor mother with several children at home for her little boy, to scare the birds from daybreak to sunset on a cold spring day off the lately sown field. From 6d. to 5s. would represent the earnings per week of boyhood up to eighteen years of age.

(1863)

33 '*Children by a pond at Fulham*', *by C. Hunt, 1859*

34 *Harvest Home, 1843. The annual feast for tenants and farm-workers in the Squire's barn*

35 *Michaelmas Goose Fair, 1873*

36   *The first English touring cricket team on their way to America, 1859*

37   *Hyde Park in the Season, 1870*

38   *Eton and Harrow Match, 1880, from a drawing by George du Maurier*

39 'The Music Lesson', a photograph of about 1857

Cook's Tours

The trip to Edinburgh, and the shorter excursions in England, attract tradesmen and their wives, merchants, clerks, away for a week's holiday, roughing it with a knapsack, and getting over an immense number of miles before they return; swarthy mechanics, who seem never able entirely to free themselves from the traces of their life-long labour, but...are by no means the worse informed, and are generally the most interested about the places they visit....As to the Swiss excursions, the company is of a very different order; the Whitsuntide trip has a good deal of the Cockney element in it, and is mostly composed of very high-spirited people, whose greatest delight in life is 'having a fling'. ...From these roysterers the July and September excursionists differ greatly; ushers and governesses, practical people from the provinces, and representatives of the better style of the London mercantile community, who form their component parts, all travel as if impressed with the notion that they are engaged in fulfilling the wishes of a lifetime, in a pleasant duty never to be repeated. They stop at all the principal towns, visiting all the curiosities to be seen in them, and are full of discussion among themselves, proving that they are all thoroughly well up in the subject. Many of them carry books of reference with them, and nearly all take notes.   (1864)

97

Addressing ourselves...to discern the inner impulse and temper of our modern art, I would say that its first characteristic is its compassionateness—its various human sympathy even warping it away from its own proper sources of power, and turning the muse of painting into a sister of charity. And this is especially shown in the importance which subjects exhibiting the life of the humbler classes have assumed, and by the delicate treatment of these. For in older art poverty was only studied for its picturesqueness—now it is tenderly watched for its mental character; of old we painted only the rags of the poor—but now, their distress. For indeed, though there never was a period in which that distress was more wantonly and widely inflicted by carelessness, there also never was a period in which it was so faithfully and brotherly pitied and helped, when it is truly discerned. The sentence 89

7

Society which Eugène Sue takes for his text in the *Mysteries of Paris*—'Si les Riches savaient'—is indeed the key to all our error and cruelty—'If the Rich only knew'.

Then the second characteristic is domesticity. All previous art contemplated men in their public aspect, and expressed only their public thought. But our art paints their home aspect, and reveals their home thoughts. Old art waited reverently in the forum. Ours plays happily in the nursery; we may call it briefly—conclusively—Art of the Nest. It does not in the least appeal for appreciation to the proud civic multitude, rejoicing in procession and assembly. It appeals only to papa and mama and nurse. And these not being in general severe judges, painters must be content if a great deal of the work produced for their approbation should be ratified by their's only.

Connected with this domestic character is the third, I am sorry to say now no more quite laudable, attribute of modern work—its shallowness of thought. To be quite comfortable in your nest, you must not care too much about what is going on outside. You must be deeply interested in little things, and greatly enjoy moderate things; that is all very bright and right on one side of it, but the morals of home, like its prettiest tapestry, have a wrong side as well as a right, and when we simply transfer that phrase of home morality to art morality, and say that this art of the nest 'is deeply interested in little things and greatly enjoys moderate things', we seem to have turned our wrong side outwards. And thus while the pictures of the Middle Ages are full of intellectual matter and meaning—schools of philosophy and theology, and solemn exponents of the faiths and fears of earnest religion—we may pass furlongs of exhibition wall without receiving any idea or sentiment, other than that home-made ginger is hot in the mouth, and that it is pleasant to be out on the lawn in fine weather.

But farther—and worse. As there is in the spirit of domesticity always a sanctified littleness, there may be also a sanctified selfishness, and a very fearful one. A man will openly do an injustice for his family's sake which he would never have done for his own; and the womanly tenderness, meant by Heaven to comfort the stranger and cherish the desolate, may, in totally unconscious selfishness, passionately exhaust itself in the sweet servilities and delicious anxieties of home. To every great error there is as great an opposite error, and the fault of modesty and simplicity which is blind to every duty but that of the family, and to every need but that of the native land, has been fatally reversed by the ascetic or missionary enthusiasm which fills the convent quiet with useless virtue, and slakes the desert sands with noble blood.

90

But between these there is a state of disciplined citizenship, in which <inline type="margin_header">*Society*</inline> the household, beloved in solemn secrecy of faithfulness, is nevertheless subjected always in thought and act to the deeper duty rendered to the larger home of the state. This ideal of citizenship has been always approached in states capable either of great art or wise legislation. From this ideal we have grievously fallen; we have retracted our consciences and affections wholly under the shadow of the roof, and losing the texture and edified strength of national fellowship, have rounded our interests into petty spheres that clash together like the dissolute pebbles of the beach. To such a nation no policy is possible but one determined by chance, and no art possible but that of petty purposes and broken designs.

(1871)

98

'The times were much harder for poor folk when I was a lad, let people say what they will,' said Benjamin Hawkins [of Langley, Wiltshire]. 'Sometimes when an outstanding field rick was threshed or brought into the barn the shepherd or carter had the privilege of planting a few potatoes there and he was so overjoyed with his good fortune that he thought he had got a small farm. There was no such thing known then as planting potatoes in the field, and this made every foot of the garden ground so precious that people could not spare room for flower-beds. Some of the old women would have a flower border and raise a few pinks and roses and a little thyme and lad's love, make up the flowers into knots and nosegays, and sell them at a $\frac{1}{2}d$. apiece. The lads would buy them and stick them in their hats on Sundays.'

(1875)

99

Cambridge, 5 April 1875. I gave a dinner party on Thursday and left the preparation of most of the dinner to [Mrs Bird the cook], simply giving my orders, and everything was perfect. I got a girl in to help. ...First, [Mrs Bird] made the rolls herself (one is laid at each plate, you know, instead of bread. She makes excellent rolls). Then she made white soup, she fried twelve fillets of sole, and made the lobster sauce to go with the fish. Next we had two entrées ordered from the

College...the first...'timballes de foie gras' and then, when this was eaten and the plates changed, the second entrée, 'sweetbreads stewed with mushrooms and truffles', was passed. With these Mrs Bird had nothing to do, which gave her breathing time to dish the main dinner. She roasted the leg of mutton, boiled the turkey, made its sauce of oysters, and cooked all the vegetables, potatoes, cauliflower and celery, which go with this course. When we were through with this, she sent up the roast duck with its sauce....I hired two waiters to help Martin [the butler] and everything passed off delightfully. We had a plum pudding from College, and after that a Charlotte Russe, then cheese...and then the table was cleared for dessert. All the wine glasses, decanters, etc., were taken off, the crumbs brushed away, and then new decanters put on, and dessert plates. The waiters then handed round one dish after another, of the dessert, after which we ladies arose and left the room to the gentlemen....

Entertaining here is a great pleasure, and no trouble to the hostess.

(1875)

100

Our evening dress needs radical reform. How it happens that black cloth has come to be associated with occasions of public and private festivity in common with occasions of public and private mourning is a riddle which we must leave posterity to solve. But it is certain that in the existing state of society, Englishmen wear the same dress at an evening party and at a funeral. Nor is this all, for many a host who entertains his friends at dinner has a butler behind his chair who is dressed precisely like himself. To add to this confusion, the clergyman who rises to say grace might, until recently, have been mistaken for either. (1878)

101

On Wednesday we are all asked to see the Museum lit up for the Conversazione with electrical light. Mrs Brownlow asked me yesterday what she should wear. I told her if we consulted our best interests, we should all wrap our faces up in some kind of head covering and look out on the world with one eye. Nothing more frightfully unbecoming than the glare of electricity having ever been discovered....

(1880)

102

77, Eaton Square   *Diner du 22 mai, 1886*

Premier Service
Consommé d'Eté

*

Filets de Soles à la Bisque
Truites froides à la Russe

*

Supreme à la Royale
Escalopes d'Agneau à la Clamart

*

Chapons poëlés à l'Andalouse

Second Service
Cailles rôties au Cressons
Haricots verts au Velouté
Œufs de Pluviers garnis d'une Salade d'Asperges

*

Mousselines à l'Ananas
Dame blanches aux Fraises

*

Petites crêmes à la Romaine

103

Mr T., Margaret Place, Gascoign Place, Bethnal Green, is a bootmaker by trade. Is a good hand, and has earned 3*s.* 6*d.* a day. He was taken ill last Christmas, and went to the London Hospital; was there three months. A week after he had gone Mrs T. had rheumatic fever, and was taken to Bethnal Green Infirmary, where she remained about three months. Directly after they had been taken ill, their furniture was seized for the three weeks' rent which was owing. Consequently, on becoming convalescent, they were homeless....He then had 2*d.*, and she had 6*d.*, which a nurse had given her....Next day he had a day's work and got 2*s.* 6*d.*, and on the strength of this they took a furnished room at 10*d.* per day (payable nightly). His work lasted a few weeks, when he was again taken ill, lost his job and spent all their money. Pawned a shirt and apron for 1*s.*; spent that too. At last pawned their tools for 3*s.*, which got them a few days' food and lodging. He is now minus tools and cannot work at his own job, and does anything he can. Spent their last 2*d.* on a pen'orth each of tea and sugar.

(1890)

104

The intelligent-looking elderly man, who was just fixing himself up on a seat [on the Embankment], informed me that he frequently made that his night's abode. 'You see,' quoth he, 'there's nowhere else so comfortable. I was here last night, and Monday and Tuesday as well, that's four nights this week. I had no money for lodgings, couldn't earn any, try as I might. I've had one bit of bread today, nothing else whatever, and I've earned nothing today or yesterday; I had 3*d.* the day before. Gets my living by carrying parcels, or minding horses, or odd jobs of that sort. You see I haven't got my health, that's where it is. I used to work on the London General Omnibus Company and after that on the Road Car Company, but I had to go to the infirmary with bronchitis and couldn't get work after that.' (1890)

105

There are still a large number of Londoners and a considerable percentage of wanderers from the country in search of work, who find themselves at nightfall destitute. These now betake themselves to the seats under the plane trees on the Embankment. Formerly they endeavoured to occupy all the seats, but the lynx-eyed Metropolitan Police declined to allow any such proceeding, and the dossers, knowing the invariable kindness of the City Police, made tracks for that portion of the Embankment which, lying east of the Temple, comes under the control of the Civic Fathers. Here, between the Temple and Black-

40   '*Blue Gate Fields, London,*' *by Gustave Doré*

41 *'Whip-behind', from 'Guttersnipes' by Phil May, 1896*

friars, I found the poor wretches by the score; almost every seat contained its full complement of six—some men, some women—all re-
clining in various postures and nearly all fast asleep....Here on the
stone abutments, which afford a slight protection from the biting wind,
are scores of men lying side by side, huddled together for warmth, and,
of course, without any other covering than their ordinary clothing....
Some have laid down a few pieces of waste paper, by way of taking the
chill off the stones, but the majority are too tired, even for that, and
the nightly toilet of most consists of first removing the hat, swathing
the head in whatever old rag may be doing duty as a handkerchief, and
then replacing the hat.   (1890)

106

It must have been in 1890 that we went to live 'over the shop'....
Below, in the basement, was a huge kitchen, with cellars behind
where some of the pledges were stored—not very interesting ones, we
thought—fenders, fire-irons, tool-boxes, spades, and the like. On the
ground floor was the shop, a long narrow place, everlastingly gaslit and
festooned with unredeemed pledges of all kinds, where Dad, with two
assistants and two or three apprentices, carried on his business of
pawnbroker and jeweller.

On the first floor were the family sitting-room and bed-rooms, and
above, in the attics, were two warehouses, one for clothing and the
other—a fascinating place to us—for ornaments, curios, and musical
instruments....

The shop itself we saw less of, though all our lives revolved round it.
From Monday to Friday it was open from 8 a.m. until 8 p.m. and on
Saturdays it never closed before 11 p.m., while often work went on up
till almost midnight. The apprentices no longer lived in—my father
during his apprenticeship had slept under the counter in the traditional
way—but they were almost part of the family, having a hasty dinner
with us in the kitchen, still in their shirtsleeves and shiny black aprons,
between spells of 'watching the shop', for there was no midday closing
then.

The shop had two entrances, one leading to the sales counter, which
was open, and the other to the pledge counter, which was divided off
by partitions so that shy customers could not see one another. At one

end of the pledge counter was a desk where one of the assistants made out pawntickets in duplicate, one ticket for the client and the other for an apprentice to pin or stick to the pledge, and entered each transaction in a huge ledger. And behind the counter stood huge racks: in these the bundles of clothing, carefully wrapped in dust sheets and bearing on one end their numbered tickets, were ranged in order, and when the racks were full the apprentices carried them up to the warehouse in the attic.

Saturday nights and Monday mornings were, of course, the busiest times. On Mondays the women brought in their family's Sunday best —the husband's suit, boots and often his watch and chain, the girls' frocks, the boys' sailor suits, their own dresses, shoes and shawls—and commonly the whole of the family wash, clean, dried and ironed, for storage until the next week-end.

Most of these things were carefully folded and wrapped in dust sheets, but (for an extra penny) dresses could be put on a hanger. I never remember seeing a hat brought in, though during the week temporarily embarrassed housewives would come with all kinds of other things—clocks, ornaments and pieces of furniture, sheets, rugs, carpets, and blankets, even wedding rings and flat-irons.   (1890)

107

Last week down our alley came a toff,
Nice old geezer with a nasty cough,
Sees my Missus, takes 'is topper off
   In a very gentlemanly way!
'Ma'am,' says 'e, 'I 'ave some news to tell,
Your rich Uncle Tom of Camberwell
Popped off recent, which it ain't a sell,
   Leavin' you 'is little Donkey Shay.'

'Wot cher!' all the neighbours cried,
   'Who're yer goin' to meet, Bill?
    Have yer bought the street, Bill?'
Laugh! I thought I should 'ave died,
   Knocked 'em in the Old Kent Road!

Some says nasty things about the moke,
One cove thinks 'is leg is really broke,
That's 'is envy, cos we're carriage folk,
    Like the toffs as rides in Rotten Row!
Straight! It woke the alley up a bit,
Thought our lodger would 'ave 'ad a fit,
When my Missus, who's a real wit,
    Says, 'I 'ates a Bus, because it's low!'

When we starts the blessed donkey stops,
'E won't move, so out I quickly 'ops,
Pals start whackin' 'im when down 'e drops,
    Someone says 'e wasn't made to go.
Lor, it might have been a four-in-'and,
My Old Dutch knows 'ow to do the grand,
First she bows, and then she waves 'er 'and,
    Callin' out, 'We're goin' for a blow!'

Ev'ry evenin' on the stroke of five
Me and Missus takes a little drive,
You'd say 'Wonderful they're still alive,'
    If you saw that little donkey go.
I soon showed 'im that 'e'd 'ave to do
Just whatever 'e was wanted to,
Still I shan't forget that rowdy crew,
    'Ollerin', 'Woa! steady! Neddy woa!'

                                  (*c.* 1892)

108

What is a fair housekeeping allowance? This depends to a great extent upon circumstances, but, roughly speaking, for a family of six or more persons, an average of £1 per head [a week] allows of luxurious living; 15*s.* per head for good living; 10*s.* for nice catering of a simple description; and 8*s.* 6*d.* per head for a sufficiency of wholesome food....

The butcher's account is apt to assume undue proportions unless great care is exercised. Those folk who must not exceed the 10*s.* a week limit should patronize American and New Zealand meat....The price of American beef has risen of late, but even now the difference between it and English beef is ½*d*. to 1*d*. the lb. This may seem but little, but it will make the difference of about 1*s*. a week in the beef bill alone for a family of eight. The difference in price between home grown and New Zealand mutton is 6½*d*. a lb. against 11½*d*. for Welsh and 10½*d*. and 11*d*. for Scotch mutton....

It will be seen...that there has not been meat for [the servants'] supper every evening, for it is not always possible to allow regular meat suppers on the 10*s*. a week allowance. If maid-servants are told of this when engaged they seldom make any objection. The domestics should be permitted to finish soup, savoury, puddings and vegetables left from late dinner, unless, of course, sufficient remains to serve again at luncheon. To supplement this fare, cocoa, milk, bread and cheese, or plain cake (if liked) should be allowed. These hints on kitchen catering only apply to families who employ two to four maid-servants. In larger establishments where there are men, or upper female servants, meat suppers are always expected....

Now that the parcel post rates are so moderate it pays the dwellers in London or other large towns to have fowls sent from Ireland. There are several dealers who will supply plump fowls of fair size at 4*s*. the couple, carriage paid, whereas in London 2*s*. 9*d*. or 3*s*. is charged for one bird of the same size. (*c.* 1898)

109

In [the kitchens of Windsor Castle] were prepared every day the meals for all the lower servants, as well as the breakfasts and ten- or twelve-course luncheons and dinners served to the Queen, the Royal Family, their guests, the lords and ladies-in-waiting who were in residence. I had expected to see one Chef in white overall and magnificent chef's toque, but there were eighteen of these men besides M. Ménager the Royal Chef, eight of them with their own tables in various parts of the kitchen.

They were assisted by the heads of various other sections, the two pastrycooks, two roast cooks, bakers, confectioners' chefs and two larder cooks. Then, in diminishing order of importance, came two assistant chefs, eight kitchen-maids, six scullery maids, six scourers, and, finally, the four apprentices. (1898)

[At Belvoir] the gong man was an old retainer, one of those numberless ranks of domestic servants which have completely disappeared. He was admittedly very old. He wore a white beard to his waist. Three times a day he rang the gong—for luncheon, for dressing time, for dinner. He would walk down the interminable passages, his livery hanging a little loosely on his bent old bones, clutching his gong with one hand and with the other feebly brandishing the padded-knobbed stick with which he struck it. Every corridor had to be warned and the towers too, so I suppose he banged on and off for ten minutes, thrice daily.

Then there were the lamp-and-candle men, at least three of them, for there was no other form of lighting, gas was despised, I forget why —vulgar, I think. They polished and scraped the wax off the candelabra, cut wicks, poured paraffin oil and unblackened glass chimneys all day long. After dark they were busy turning wicks up or down, snuffing candles, and de-waxing extinguishers....

The water-men are difficult to believe in today. They seemed to me to belong to another clay. They were the biggest people I had ever seen, much bigger than any of the men of the family, who were remarkable for their height. They had stubbly beards and a general Bill Sikes appearance. They wore brown clothes, no collars and thick green baize aprons from chin to knee. On their shoulders they carried a wooden yoke from which hung two gigantic cans of water. They moved on a perpetual round. Above the ground floor there was no drop of hot water and not one bath, so their job was to keep all jugs, cans and kettles full in the bedrooms, and morning and evening to bring the hot water for the hip-baths. [As children] we were always a little frightened of the water-men. They seemed of another element and never spoke but one word, 'Water-man', to account for themselves.

If anyone had the nerve to be abed until 11 o'clock...there were many strange callers at the door. First the housemaid, scouring the steel grate and encouraging the fire of the night before, which always burned until morning, and refilling the kettle on the hob until it sang again. Next the unearthly water-giants. Then a muffled knock given by the knee, for the coalman's hands were too dirty and too full. He was a sinister man, much like his brothers of the water, but blacker far and generally more mineral. He growled the single word 'Coalman' and refilled one's bin with pieces the size of ice-blocks....

Lastly there were the watchmen, who frightened many a newcomer   101 to death. There was a little of the water-men about them, but they were dreadfully silent and they padded. All night they walked the passages, terraces and battlements, yet no one really saw them.... Always if one woke in the night, as the fire flickered to its death, one would hear a padded foot on the gravel outside and a voice, not loud enough to waken, but strong enough to reassure, saying 'Past 12 o'clock. All's well.'

(*c.* 1899)

111

The scene in...Hyde Park, on fine afternoons, is most interesting and imposing. In the Drive are seen unbroken files of elegant equipages and high-bred horses in handsome trappings moving continually to and fro, presided over by sleek coachmen and powdered lackeys, and occupied by some of the most beautiful and exquisitely dressed women in the world. In the Row are numerous riders, who parade their spirited and glossy steeds before the admiring crowd sitting or walking at the sides.

(1900)

112

The Duchess of Sutherland's concert for the Highland Brigade on Wednesday evening was the event of the week and was a brilliant success. It took place at the Queen's Hall. The Duchess gave a large dinner party at Stafford House before the concert, at which were present Lady Buchan and the Ladies Erskine, Lady Constance Mackenzie, Miss Chaplin, Mr Balfour, Mr Munro Ferguson, and Mr Harry Henderson. Lady Napier of Magdala, Princess Alexis Dolgorouky, and many others also had parties. The Grand Duchess of Coburg and Princess Henry of Battenberg were received by Lord Balfour of Burleigh, Secretary for Scotland and Mr Harry Henderson, honorary secretary for the concert, at the Royal entrance, and conducted to the State chairs specially brought from Stafford House. The young ladies selling the programmes, which included a lovely sketch by Princess Louise Duchess of Argyll of 'The Girl I Left Behind Me', in white dresses, tartan sashes, and white satin swords, were a gathering of all the beauties of the season. The Duchess of Coburg and Princess Henry remained quite to the end, and thoroughly enjoyed the entertainment.

(1900)

WOMEN

42 *From a drawing by George du Maurier, 1880*

The 'Annuals' nominally edited by Lady Blessington—the *Book of Beauty* from 1834 to 1847, and the *Keepsake* from 1841 to 1849—still dominate our idea of Early Victorian woman: young, large-eyed, ringleted, melting, beautiful beyond probability. The legal facts of her life were rather less delightful. A wife separated from her husband—on whatever grounds—had no right of access to her children. In 1838 a Bill was brought in to allow her, if she were 'of irreproachable conduct', to see them by petition to the Equity Judges, who were to regulate the terms of access. The Bill was passed in the Commons; but Brougham opposed it in the Lords, partly on the grounds that women suffered so much under the law that it was foolish to amend one small item of hardship. The Bill was duly thrown out. **103**

Married women could own no property, though they could benefit under a trust. Charlotte Brontë found with a certain surprise, after her marriage to her father's curate in 1854, that the ownership and direction of her copyrights, and the enjoyment of her royalties, had passed to her husband.

It was only when Florence Nightingale was thirty-three, and her father gave her an allowance of £500 a year, that she could begin to do what she wanted in gaining experience of nursing. Before then she had been the slave not only of convention, not only of her family's selfish ideas of her duty to them, but also of her financial dependence on their whims. It must be remembered, too, that she succeeded in getting Army nursing reformed not merely by force of character but also—and more effectively—by knowing the right people. The Minister for War, whoever he might be, was always an old friend. Mrs Gladstone, a pious woman much given to good works, found it quite natural to refuse permission to her daughter Agnes to train as a nurse, because, at twenty-nine, she was far too young. Agnes was in fact useful at home.

The daughter was subordinate; the wife was hardly ever the equal of her husband. By contrast such memoirs as Augustus Hare's depict a snobbish clerical society ruled by strong-minded and rich widows. To be a widow with a good social position and a good jointure was, indeed, to be well-placed in upper-middle-class society. The 'Widow of Windsor' was the Queen of a great many other widows; some of them wise and kind, and remembered to this day with reverent affection by their descendants, but too many of them conventional, powerful, stupid and even cruel.

The Victorian Age saw the gradual emancipation of women, in the years after 1857. In that year the Divorce Act transferred the hearing of matrimonial causes from the ecclesiastical courts to a new secular court. Divorce was to be granted on the adultery of a wife, and on adultery and cruelty by a husband; it still conferred a disreputable stigma even on the innocent spouse.

In 1865 Elizabeth Garrett, a woman of twenty-nine, member of a distinguished dissenting family, after many struggles secured the licence of the Society of Apothecaries to practise medicine. In 1869 Madame Bodichon and Miss Emily Davies established a house for women students at Hitchin, which in 1873 became Girton College. In 1871 (the year in which the Religious Test was abolished in English universities) Miss Clough opened the house of residence at Cambridge that was later to become Newnham College. In 1879 Somerville and

Lady Margaret Hall were established at Oxford. Though women students could attend most university lectures, be tutored by dons, and take the men's examinations, they could not be admitted to degrees.

The great change in the position of women came with the Married Women's Property Act of 1881. Before that, any wife's property (unless protected by a trust, that implicitly denied her any control over it) belonged to her husband.

43 'Garden Flowers', by W. P. Frith

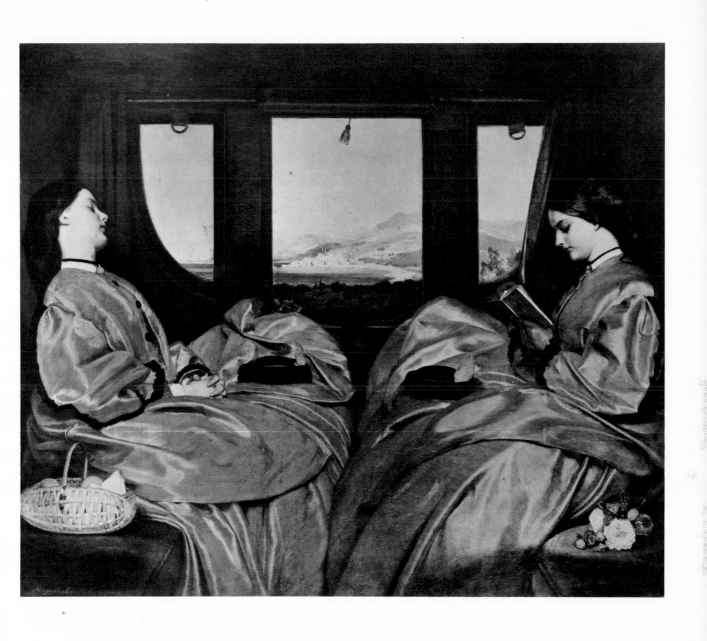

45 *'The Travelling Companions', by Augustus Egg, 1862*

46 *'The Widow's Mite', by J. E. Millais*

Sarah and Eliza were in good-natured rapture over the whole [trousseau], from the Brussels lace wedding gown to the very last dozen of embroidered pocket handkerchiefs....

'Thirty morning gowns,' whispered Sarah as they went downstairs. 'The idea of a new gown every day for a month; now I call that real happiness.'

'Not such real, lasting happiness', answered Eliza, 'as eighteen bracelets, then those heaps of gloves and handkerchiefs. A quarter of them, Sarah, would free our miserable allowances from embarrassments for life.'

'It must be very pleasant to be so rich—'

'And to be going to be married,' said Eliza; and this sage conclusion brought them to the drawing-room door. (*c.* 1830)

114

The sentiment for woman has undergone a change. The romantic passion, which once almost deified her, is on the decline; and it is by intrinsic qualities that she must now inspire respect.

A woman may make a man's home delightful, and may thus increase his motives for virtuous exertion. She may refine and tranquillize his mind—may turn away his anger, or allay his grief. Where want of congeniality impairs domestic comfort, the fault is generally chargeable on the female side; for it is for woman, not for man, to make the sacrifice, especially in indifferent matters. She must, in a certain degree, be plastic herself, if she would mould others, and this is one reason why very good women are sometimes very uninfluential. They do a great deal, but they yield nothing....

In everything that women attempt, they should show their consciousness of dependence. There is something so unpleasant in female self-sufficiency, that it not infrequently prejudices instead of persuading.

Their sex should ever teach them to be subordinate; and they should remember that, by them, influence is to be obtained, not by assumption, but by a delicate appeal to affection or principle. Women, in this respect, are something like children: the more they show their need of support, the more engaging they are.

The *bas bleu* is eager for notoriety, and avails herself of her requirements only to secure it. She does all she can to sustain her claims; she
accumulates around her the materials of learning, and her very boudoir
breathes an academic air. Its decorations are sufficient to proclaim
her character; its shelves are filled with books of every tongue; its
tables are strewed with the apparatus of science; the casket of jewels
is displaced for the cabinet of stones, and the hammer and alembic
occupy the stand allotted for the workbox. One niche glooms with a
quartered skull; another is enriched by a classic statue; the easel
stands in the background, and the harp is admitted to complete the
picturesque. And she herself is in accordance with all this parapher-
nalia; and her conversation, dress and manner equally attest her
eagerness to make good her pretensions to literary notoriety.

(?1837)

115

Amongst other things I saw a cotton mill....The place was full of
women, young, all of them, some large with child, and obliged to stand
twelve hours each day. Their hours are from 5 in the morning to 7 in
the evening, two hours of that being for rest....The heat was excessive
in some of the rooms, the stink pestiferous, and in all an atmosphere of
cotton flue. I nearly fainted. The young women were all pale, sallow,
thin, yet generally fairly grown, all with bare feet—a strange sight to
English eyes. By the by, it rained all day nearly, and in every gutter
you might see rows of children standing to wash their feet. They looked
like so many strings of young ducks. (1839)

116

8 June 1839. I have striven hard to be pleased with my new situation
[as governess at Mr John Sidgwick's, Stonegappe]. The country, the
house, and the grounds are as I have said, divine; but, alack-a-day,
there is such a thing as seeing all beautiful around you—pleasant
woods, white paths, green lawns, and blue sunshiny sky—and not
having a free moment or a free thought left to enjoy them. The children
are constantly with me. As for correcting them, I quickly found that
110 was out of the question; they are to do as they like. A complaint to

the mother only brings black looks on myself, and unjust partial excuses to screen the children.... I said in my last letter that Mrs Sidgwick did not know me. I now begin to find she does not intend to know me: that she cares nothing about me except to contrive how the greatest possible quantity of labour may be got out of me, and to that end she overwhelms me with oceans of needlework; yards of cambric to hem, muslin nightcaps to make, and above all things, dolls to dress.... I see more clearly than I have ever done before that a private governess has no existence, is not considered as a living rational being, except as connected with the wearisome duties she has to fulfil.

(1839)

117

Man for the field and woman for the hearth;
Man for the sword and for the needle she;
Man with the head and woman with the heart;
Man to command and woman to obey;
All else confusion.

(1847)

118

Jane Eyre is throughout the personification of an unregenerate and undisciplined spirit.... Altogether the autobiography of Jane Eyre is pre-eminently an anti-Christian composition. There is throughout it a murmuring against the comforts of the rich and against the privations of the poor, which is a murmuring of God's appointment—there is a proud and perpetual assertion of the rights of man, for which we find no authority in God's word or in God's providence. We do not hesitate to say that the tone of mind and thought which has overthrown and violated every code human and divine abroad and fostered Chartism and rebellion at home, is the same which has also written *Jane Eyre*.

(1847)

119

O weary days—oh evenings that seem never to end—for how many years have I watched that drawing-room clock and thought it would never reach the ten! and for twenty, thirty years more to do this!...

Women Women don't consider themselves as human beings at all. There is absolutely no God, no country, no duty to them at all, except family ...I have known a good deal of convents, and of course everyone has talked of the petty grinding tyrannies supposed to be exercised there, but I know nothing like the petty grinding tyranny of a good English family. And the only alleviation is that the tyrannized submits with a heart full of affection. (1851)

120

From Committees, Charity and Schism, from the Church of England, from philanthropy and all deceits of the devil, good Lord deliver us.
(1853)

121

Your daughters, perhaps, have been seized with the prevailing 'Pteri-domania', and are collecting and buying ferns, with Ward's cases wherein to keep them (for which you have to pay) and wrangling over unpronounceable names of species (which seem to be different in each new Fern-book that they buy), till the Pteridomania seems to you something of a bore; and yet you cannot deny that they find an en-joyment in it, and are more active, more cheerful, more self-forgetful over it, than they would have been over novels and gossip, crochet and Berlin wool. (1855)

122

I would earnestly ask my sisters to keep clear of both the jargons now current everywhere...of the jargon, namely, about the 'rights' of women, which urges women to do all that men do, including the medi-cal and other professions, merely because men do it...and of the jargon which urges women to do nothing that men do, merely because they are women....

You do not want the effect of your good things to be, 'How wonder-ful for a *woman*!' nor would you be deterred from good things, by hearing it said, 'Yes, but she ought not to have done this, because it is not suitable for a woman'. But you want to do the thing that is

good, whether it is 'suitable for a woman' or not. (1860)

47   *A window fernery and fountain*

48 *Family photograph: Mother and the girls, c. 1865*

49   *A game of tennis. Flowing clothes held in by embroidered aprons.*
By George du Maurier, 1880

50   *The first women students to be admitted to lectures at the University of Cambridge, photographed at Hitchin, 1869*

It is often said by men, that it is unwise to teach women anything
about these laws of health, because they will take to physicking—
that there is a great deal too much of amateur physicking as it is,
which is indeed true....There is nothing ever seen in any professional
practice like the reckless physicking by amateur females....To cultivate in things pertaining to health observation and experience in
women who are mothers, governesses or nurses, is just the way to do
away with amateur physicking....

It is often said by women that they cannot know anything of the
laws of health...because they can know nothing of 'Pathology', or
cannot 'dissect'.   (1860)

124

I have always thought that there is no more fruitful source of family
discontent than a housewife's badly cooked dinners and untidy ways.
Men are so well-served out of doors—in their well-ordered taverns and
dining-places—that in order to compete with the attractions of these
places a mistress must be thoroughly acquainted with the theory and
practice of cookery as well as be perfectly conversant with all the other
arts of making and keeping a comfortable home.   (1861)

125

The application of a little knowledge of the world and common sense
to the case of the angry parents who consider it shameful that their
young daughters cannot frequent Oxford and Regent Streets without
the risk of being spoken to by 'miscreants', may possibly relieve you
and the public from future appeals of a similar nature. I fear that in
London, as in all other great cities, young and good-looking girls will
always require a companion in public places frequented by young and
good-looking men if they desire to be secure from interruption.

All fathers of families are like 'Paterfamilias from the Country',
quite certain that their daughters are perfectly demure and well be-
haved, until they have conclusive proof to the contrary. They forget
the private history of their own youth; they cannot believe that **117**

Blanche ever looked kindly at a strange *joli garçon* who appeared struck with her appearance; or that Isabel ever designedly showed rather more than her very neat ankle to a young officer in crossing a street. It never occurs to them that bonnets of the 'kiss me quick' build, loud stockings, exaggerated tournures, capes and crinolines, vagrant ringlets straying over the shoulder, better known by the name of 'follow me, lads', and suchlike decoys, are all unmistakeably intended to attract the notice and attentions of the male sex.   (1862)

126

I have long sought for some instances of invention or discovery by a woman. And the best I have been able to find is Thwaites's soda-water. A Miss Thwaites of Dublin, an amateur chemist, hit on an improvement in soda-water, which enabled her to drive all others out of the market. But besides this, some small musical compositions, and some pretty novels and poems, are all the female inventions I can find.

(1864)

127

Could not the existing disabilities as to property and influence of women be swept away by the legislature as it stands at present?... Till a married woman can be in possession of her own property there can be no love or justice....Is it possible that, if woman suffrage is agitated as a means of removing these evils, the effect may be to prolong their existence?   (1867)

128

I am obliged to you for your letter respecting the proposed College for Ladies, but as I have decided objections to bringing large masses of girls together and think that home education under the inspection and encouragement of sensible fathers, or voluntarily continued by the girls themselves, is far more valuable, both intellectually and morally than any external education, I am afraid I cannot assist you.

I feel with much regret that female education is deficient, but I think the way to meet the evil is by rousing the parents to lead their

daughters to read, think, and converse. All the most superior women
I have known have thus been formed by *home* influence, and I think
that girls in large numbers always hurt one another in manner and
tone if in nothing else.   (1868)

129

Exposure of the face is one of the great tendencies of the time; and
though it is not exactly indelicate in itself, yet the bold confronting of
notice that is involved in going out with a totally unprotected countenance, thrown into prominence on the headdress, cannot be modest in
itself; nor does a veil coming close over the nose materially alter the
matter. Many perfectly retiring quiet girls adopt it simply from custom, and their refined faces cannot be entirely spoilt by it; but when
the same hat is perched on a coarse face the evil of the example is
apparent.   (*c.* 1870)

130

None of the other girls had any special tasks. The laborious expensive
education of their childhood did not lead to anything worth the name
of a pursuit, much less a hobby, with any one of them. Of the happiness of learning, of the exciting interest of an intellectual hobby, they
knew nothing. With much pains and labour they had been drilled in
arts and sciences, in languages and 'the usual branches of an English
education'. But apart from social duties and amusements, the chief
occupation of their lives was needlework....

   In vain had 'the first masters' made my cousins glib in chromatic
passages, and dexterous with tricks of effects in colours and crayons.
They played duets after dinner and Aunt Maria sometimes showed off
the water-colour copies of their schoolroom days, which, indeed, they
now and then recopied for bazaars; but for their own pleasure they
never touched a note or a pencil.   (1873)

131

It had been announced that the Civil Service Commissioners would
receive applications personally [at Cannon Row] from candidates for
eleven vacancies in the metropolitan post offices, and in answer to this

notice, about 2000 young women made their appearance....Many of the applicants, it appears, were girls of the highest respectability and of unusually good social position, including daughters of clergymen and professional men, well connected, well educated, tenderly nurtured; but never the less driven by the *res angustae* which have caused many a heartbreak...to seek the means of independent support.... The Commissioners examined over 1000 candidates for the eleven vacancies. This seems a sad waste of power on both sides, when, in all probability, the first score supplied the requisite number of qualified aspirants. (1873)

132

Nurse Q.:   prim little body.

Miss W.:   poor creature.

Nurse G.:   makings of a nice nurse, no pretensions, most willing, good in ward.

Nurse M.:   good influence, quiet and religious.

Miss B.:   Lydia Languish.

Nurse N.:   hoyden, vulgar, slangy, so ill brought up.

Nurse W.:   useful little body; rather bright and perky.

Nurse S.:   green young saint.

(1875)

133

The faculty of distinguishing good from bad design in the familiar objects of domestic life is a faculty which most educated people—and women especially—conceive that they possess....The general impression seems to be, that it is the peculiar inheritance of gentle blood, and independent of all training; that, while a young lady is devoting at school or under a governess, so many hours a day to music, so many to languages, and so many to general science, she is all this time unconsciously forming that sense of the beautiful, which we call taste: that this sense, once developed, will enable her, unassisted by special study or experience, not only to appreciate the charms of nature in every aspect, but to form a correct estimate of the merits of art-manufacture. (1878)

EDUCATION

51 *Harrow School Room, a drawing by* **T. W. Pugin**

Education, at the beginning of the Victorian era, was fundamentally a classical education. The fact not only made the education of those who by birth and circumstance were considered incapable of Greek and Latin relatively unimportant but also made the curriculum of the public schools extremely restricted. Arnold at Rugby in 1840 naturally made the classical languages the basis of the whole curriculum. He admitted French and German, but had them taught as dead languages, with no attempt to teach pronunciation and no aim but to make it possible to read texts. Lord Derby, a man of more European culture, protested, as a Governor, but was told that boys at an English school would never learn to speak or pronounce French.

Education, for all but the last years of the reign, was in the hands of parsons. As Fellows they controlled the universities; as headmasters **121** they controlled the public and grammar schools; as incumbents they controlled the elementary schools.

At the beginning of Queen Victoria's reign these last had lately increased in number, for in 1834 the Government had voted £20,000 towards the erection of school-houses. The grant was to be used to meet half the cost, the rest to be met by voluntary subscription through the National or British and Foreign School Societies. The grant was primarily intended for the large towns and was renewed annually for the next six years. Some 714 Anglican National Schools and some 181 undenominational British Schools were erected.

There was need of them. In 1841, 33 per cent of men and 49 per cent of women marrying in England could only sign the register with a mark; in 1853 the figures had dropped only to 31 and 45 per cent. London and Middlesex were the most literate; Monmouth and Bedfordshire the least. The Commission of 1859 on Elementary Education was entirely justified. In 1865, for the first time, over a million English children were attending elementary schools; in most instances their parents paid a few pence a week for the privilege. They were taught 'the three R's—Reading, 'Riting, and 'Rithmetic'—rather well; and the girls were generally instructed in good plain stitchery, sometimes to the mistress's profit.

In 1870 the debates on the Elementary Education Bill revealed that there might be an average daily attendance at elementary schools of a million, but that only two-thirds of the children between six and ten attended, and only one-third of those between ten and twelve. A quarter of the children of Liverpool between five and thirteen never entered a school, and conditions at Manchester, Leeds and Birmingham were little better. When in that year Huxley, as a member of the London School Board, said 'I conceive it to be our duty to make a ladder from the gutter to the university along which any child may climb', he was speaking as an idealist and was condemned as unpractical.

1870 was a significant year. Forster's Act created Board Schools to supplement the Voluntary Schools, and Cowper-Temple's Amendment forbade denominational teaching in rate-aided schools. Furthermore women became eligible as members of school boards. By 1886 there were over 3 million elementary school 'places', about half by 'voluntary'—that is, Anglican—agency, and about half by secular authority.

Such grammar schools as did not, like Rugby, move into the public school class, made comparatively little progress in Victorian times. To

send an occasional undergraduate to Oxford or Cambridge from their endowments, with a view to taking Orders, continued to be their chief contribution to learning. The institution of high schools for girls in 1881 opened the way to a great social development, but made little noise at the time.

A stronger wind of change blew through the universities. The foundation of London University in 1837 as an examining body, rapidly developing into the undenominational (and indeed non-professing) University College and the Anglican King's College, shook the Establishment. In 1851 the foundation of Owens College, Manchester, by a merchant of that city, began the series of foundations of provincial universities that ultimately did more than anything to break the early Victorian tradition of education. In 1854 a Catholic university was founded at Dublin. In the same year Maurice, Hughes and Ludlow founded the Working Men's College in Great Ormond Street. Such extra-mural teaching was made available to the middle classes by the institution of university extension lectures in 1867.

The older universities were in need of reform, for they no longer took learning seriously. Thomas Arnold in 1841 was offered, and found it proper to accept, the chair of the Regius Professor of Modern History at Oxford, though he knew nothing of the subject; and his appointment was balanced by that of Kingsley to the Cambridge chair in 1860. At neither great university was pure knowledge held sacred.

Not everyone was satisfied. In April 1850 Lord John Russell appointed a commission to inquire into and report on the state of the universities. At Oxford the Hebdomadal Board was extremely angry, and said that the Laudian reform of 1636 had done all that was needful.

The commission began to sit in 1851; thanks to its recommendations, new professorial chairs were established, with endowments drawn from the richer colleges. Most college Fellowships were freed from their former restrictions, without losing their administrative privileges. Scholarships were greatly increased in number and value, and the religious tests required for taking the Bachelor's degree abolished; those for the M.A. were removed by the House of Lords in 1871. In 1862 the number of undergraduates at Oxford was 1526; by 1887 it had risen to 2979.

52   *A school run on the monitorial system, 1839*

53   *Dinner-time at the Clare-market Ragged School*

54   *Eton College, the Upper Grammar School, 1861*

55   *Photograph of a village school, c. 1856*

I was not six years old before my mother...began to follow out a code of penance for me....Hitherto I had never been allowed anything but roast-mutton and rice pudding for dinner. Now all was changed. The most delicious puddings were talked of—*dilated* on—until I became, not greedy, but exceedingly curious about them. At length *le grand moment* arrived. They were put on the table before me, and then, just as I was going to eat some of them, they were snatched away, and I was told to get up and carry them off to some poor person in the village.

(1839)

135

Childishness in boys, even of good abilities, seems to me to be a growing fault, and I do not know to what to ascribe it, except to the great number of exciting books of amusement, like *Pickwick* and *Nickleby*, *Bentley's Magazine*, etc., etc. These completely satisfy all the intellectual appetite of a boy, which is rarely very voracious, and leave him totally palled not only for his regular work...but for good literature of all sorts, even for history and for poetry.

(1839)

136

The position of a schoolmaster in society...has not yet obtained that respect in England, as to be able to stand by itself in public opinion as a liberal profession; it owes the rank which it holds to its connexion with the profession of a clergyman, for that is acknowledged universally in England to be the profession of a gentleman. Mere teaching, like mere literature, places a man, I think, in rather an equivocal position; he holds no undoubted station in society by these alone; for neither education nor literature have ever enjoyed that consideration and general respect in England which they enjoy in France and in Germany. But a far higher consideration is this, that he who is to educate boys, if he is fully sensible of the importance of his business, must be unwilling to lose such great opportunities as the clerical character gives him, by enabling him to address them continually from the pulpit, and to administer the Communion to them as they become old enough to receive it.

(1839)

From an Oxford correspondent

We are full of restorations and rumours of restorations. A total repair and almost rebuilding of Baliol College is in contemplation, and Mr Pugin was invited to execute it, but it has been thought inexpedient to employ a Roman Catholic, and especially a violent partizan, and the Master of Baliol has withdrawn his consent.　　　　　(1843)

138

3 December. Mr Watts...talked also of the projected large School for the Farmers—or rather College as the word now is.—As he spoke much in its favour and conceived it would equip the farmers so highly for their vocation, I ventured to press my own opinion as adverse to such a project both on political and constitutional grounds. In so exclusive and agricultural an education with a profuse smattering of the 'ologies', and a *tincture* of science and art, without the rudiments of an ingenious and classical education, you not only rear a class of cad of the farming grade and perhaps make them conceited and discontented subjects—but you prevent their aspiring and fitting themselves for the higher posts and professions of our society, and defeat the constitutional principle, that all promotion and preferment are open to the ambitions and fair efforts of every individual.　　　　(1850)

139

The proposal is, That secretaries under and upper, that all manner of changeable or permanent servants in the government offices shall be selected *without* reference to their power of getting into Parliament.... An immense accession of intellect might ensue...and the actual flower of whatever intellect the British Nation had might be attracted towards Downing Street, and continue flowing steadily thither!

(1850)

140

The ingenuity of the boys [at Radley] was taxed to the utmost to mitigate the severity of our diet. Servitors were bribed to put apples in our beds. All kinds of bulbs were dug up in the park and the gardens

and eagerly devoured. Cowslip roots were a delicacy, nasturtium,
crocuses and hyacinths did not long remain in the gardens....Acorns
were collected in great numbers and stored away in holes dug in the
park. These were secretly cooked in the flames of candles.   (*c.* 1851)

141

We have confessed likewise that...this is the only country that has
neither supplied...scientific or artistic instruction to its industrial
population; nor, for men of science and art, a centre of action, and of
exchange of the result of their labours....Yet this country, as the
centre of commerce and industry of the world, would seem to require,
more than any other, to have these wants supplied; and the Great
Exhibition has, in its results, convinced us that unless they be speedily
procured, this country will run serious risk of losing that pre-eminent
position which now makes its strength and its boast.   (1852)

142

[A university] is a place of *teaching* universal *knowledge*. This implies
that its object is, on the one hand, intellectual, not moral; and, on the
other, that it is the diffusion and extension of knowledge rather than
the advancement. If its object were scientific and philosophical discovery, I do not see why a university should have student religious
training. I do not see how it can be the seat of literature and science.
                                                              (1852)

143

Recreations are not education, accomplishments are not education.
Do not say, the people must be educated, when, after all, you only
mean amused, refreshed, soothed, put into good spirits and good
humour, or kept from vicious excesses. I do not say that such amusements, such occupations of mind, are not a great gain; but they are
not education. You may as well call drawing and fencing education,
as a general knowledge of botany or conchology. Stuffing birds or
playing stringed instruments is an elegant pastime, and a resource to
the idle, but it is not education; it does not form or cultivate the intellect. Education is a high word; it is the preparation for knowledge,
and it is the imparting of knowledge in proportion to that preparation.
                                                      (1852)

Our life [at Winchester] was certainly a narrow one in every way. We were shut off from the outside world. We were shut off from one another. We were shut off from the Masters. Masters and boys lived in different worlds. I never spoke to a Master, except officially, on school business...nor did it ever occur to me that there could be any other relation. The Masters were simply another Creation.

But the first real change in the relation began with the establishment of the first House in 1859. Still even then the Wykehamical tradition was so strong that I am assured that the first housemaster ...never went at night into his own boys' bedrooms without putting on his tall hat and overcoat. (1852–9)

145

One peculiarity in the history of our time is...[that] the most intelligent patrons of juvenile education...are very generally convinced that all our schools ought to be industrial schools....I have heard that some who have spent their lives in promoting the instruction of the poor, and whose purses are as open as ever they were, have declared that they will not give a shilling to any school in which work and teaching are not combined. Now, though I am sure that one of their objects is to prepare the children for being tailors or shoe-makers or cooks or housemaids, hereafter, I cannot believe that this is their chief object. Sullen masters or mistresses may say that they do not care for the school apprenticeships, that they could teach their servants better themselves. But the advantages of this discipline are found to be immediate, not prospective. The children may not at once earn better wages...but they do their school tasks infinitely better. Not only are their bodily powers cultivated, but the words which they read acquire a life and vitality which they scarcely ever have when the book stands by itself, when the only business is to spell it out. On the other hand, the work, even if it is imperfectly executed, is understood to be a part of the day's duties; its character is raised; and the child does not look forward to the workshop as something which is to separate him from

all that he is doing before he goes to it. (1854)

56 *Rugby School from the Close, c. 1870*

57　*St Andrew's College and Industrial Schools, Chardstock, Dorset, 1861*

58   *A group of Eton boys, c. 1890*

59   *Undergraduates at Cambridge, c. 1900*

The object of a university is not simply or mainly to cultivate the intellect. Intellect, by itself, heightened, sharpened, refined, cool, piercing, subtle, would be after the likeness, not of God, but of His enemy, who is acuter and subtler far than the acutest and subtlest. The object of universities is with and through the discipline of the intellect, as far as may be, to discipline and train the whole moral and intelligent being. The problem and special work of an [*sic*] university is, not how to advance science, not how to make discoveries, not to form new schools of mental philosophy, nor to invent new modes of analysis; not to produce works in Medicine, Jurisprudence, or even Theology; but to form minds religiously, morally, intellectually, which shall discharge aright whatever duties God, in His Providence, shall appoint to them. Acute and subtle intellects, even though well disciplined, are not needed for most offices in the body politic.... The type of the best English intellectual character is sound, solid, steady, thoughtful, patient, well-disciplined judgment. It would be a perversion of our institutions to turn the university into a forcing-house for intellect.   (1854)

147

[The] discipline which boys meet with at Eton, Winchester and Harrow, etc., is much worse than that of adult life—much more unjust, cruel, brutal. Instead of being an aid to human progress, which all culture should be, the culture of our public schools, by accustoming boys to a despotic form of government, and an intercourse regulated by brute force, tends to fit them for a lower state of society than that which exists. And chiefly recruited as our legislature is from those who are brought up at these schools, this barbarizing influence becomes a serious hindrance to national progress.   (1861)

148

A public meeting was held in the Sheldonian Theatre, Oxford, yesterday, to promote the establishment of cheap self-supporting schools for the lower middle classes, in connexion with St Nicolas College, Lancing, in Sussex. It should be stated that St Nicolas College was founded in

1848, with the special object of improving middle-class education. Besides large buildings at Lancing on a property of 230 acres, as the headquarters of the society, with a grammar school for the sons of gentlemen, the College has in operation a college at Hurstpierpoint, in Sussex, for training middle schoolmasters; a public boarding school in the same building for the upper class of tradesmen, farmers, clerks, etc., at a payment varying according to circumstances from £20 to £30 a-year, containing more than 250 boys, who are taught by seven clergymen and graduates of the universities, with six other trained masters; and a cheaper boarding school at Shoreham, for the sons of small shopkeepers and artisans, at which the payment for board and education is but 13 guineas a-year. This is carried on for the most part in houses hired by the parents of the boys, 230 of whom are already admitted, and no more houses can be hired. This disadvantage it is now sought to remedy by the erection of premises to accommodate 1000 boys, with an adequate staff of masters, on a site near Balcombe, Sussex. (1861)

149

Shall I give you some good advice? It is only this—to make yourself a good cricketer, football player, etc., and not to sit 'sapping' too much while other boys are at play. It does not answer in the long run. You want to improve your mind as well as do a certain number of lines, sums, etc. But you cannot do this unless you improve your health. The boys are not far wrong in respecting a boy who is 'good at games' and I would advise you to try and gain their respect in this way as well as in books. (1861)

150

In the recent education inquiry one of the assistant-commissioners, Mr A. F. Foster, who visited the extreme north of England, called attention to the difficulty created by the gulf between the language of the lesson-book and that of ordinary intercourse. In Teesdale, for instance, though the prevalence of education is such that the adult population generally understand any ordinary English book, they still use the local dialect as their everyday medium. It would be deemed affectation to do otherwise. Hence children find the language of books

strange for a time. 'Mother, kent t'wy an' gaid t'meenen', said an
educated lad, referring to his early difficulties in this respect, and this
youth actually interpreted his own vernacular in good English when the
commissioner did not appear to understand him. A teacher from one
of the London institutions was giving an object lesson on bread, and
supposed herself understood until a pupil-teacher ventured to inform
her that the children knew nothing about bran: their name for it was
'chizzle'. The familiar teaching of common things, however, it is
thought, may tend to bridge over the chasm between the language of
the educated and that of the vulgar. Constantly hearing the latter
out of school it takes a child a long while to gain that familiarity with
literary language which will enable it to understand an ordinary book,
sermon, or newspaper, and there seems to be no work written with a
view of introducing the child gradually and systematically to an
acquaintance with literary language.   (1861)

151

First...there should be training schools for Youth established, at
government cost and under government discipline, over the whole
country; that every child born in the country should, at the parent's
wish, be permitted (and, in certain cases, be under penalty required)
to pass through them; and that, in these schools, the child should...
imperatively be taught, with the best skill of teaching the country
could produce...
  (*a*) the laws of health and the exercises enjoined by them;
  (*b*) habits of gentleness and justice;
  (*c*) the calling by which he is to live.
  Secondly—that, in connexion with these training schools, there
should be established, also entirely under government regulation,
manufactories and workshops for the production and sale of every
necessary of life, and for the exercise of every useful art....
  Thirdly—that any man or woman, or boy, or girl, out of employment, should be at once received at the nearest government school,
and set to such work as it appeared, on trial, they were fit for, at a
fixed rate of wages determined every year....
  Lastly—that for the old and destitute comfort and home should be
provided, which provision...would be honourable instead of dis-
graceful to the receiver.   (1862)   137

The colleges no longer promote the researches of science, or direct professional study. Here and there college walls may shelter an occasional student, but not in larger proportions than may be found in private life. Elementary teaching of youths under twenty-two is now the only function performed by the university, and almost the only object of college endowments. (1868)

153

The scholar's gown is too often to be found on youths who have no vocation for science or literature and whom it was no kindness to have drawn away from their proper destination to active life. They have come here as a commercial speculation. High wages are given for learning Latin and Greek and they are sent to enlist to earn the pay. (1868)

154

Spoiled by the luxury of home and early habits of self-indulgence, the young aristocrat has lost the power of commanding the attention, and is not only indisposed for, but incapable of, work....He is either the foppish exquisite of the drawing-room, or the barbarized athlete of the arena, and beyond these spheres all life to him is a blank. (1868)

155

I have no patience with the hypothesis occasionally expressed, and often implied, especially in tales written to teach children to be good, that babies are born pretty much alike, and that the sole agencies in creating differences between boy and boy, and man and man, are steady application and moral effort. It is in the most unqualified manner that I object to pretensions of natural equality. The experiences of the nursery, the school, the university, and of professional careers, are a chain of proofs to the contrary. (1870)

156

I have not dared to occupy myself much with people whose gifts are below the average, but they would be an interesting study. The number of idiots and imbeciles among the 20 million inhabitants of England and Wales is approximately estimated at 50,000 or as 1 in 400....I know two good instances of hereditary silliness, short of imbecility, and have reason to believe I could easily obtain a large number of similar facts. (1870)

157

Natural Science is now occupying a more and more important place in education. Oxford, Cambridge, the London University, the public schools, one after another, are taking up the subject in earnest; so are the middle-class schools; so, I trust, will all primary schools throughout the country; and I hope that my children, at least, if not I myself, will see the day, when ignorance of the primary laws and facts of science will be looked on as a defect, only second to ignorance of the primary laws of religion and morality. (1873)

158

There is a branch of education in which, even now, the poor man can compete fairly against the rich; and that is, Natural Science. In the first place, the rich, blind to their own interests, have neglected it hitherto in their schools, so that they have not the start of the poor man on that subject which they have on many. In the next place, Natural Science is a subject which a man cannot learn by paying for teachers. He must teach it himself by patient observation, by patient common sense. And if the poor man is not the rich man's equal in those qualities, it must be his own fault, not his purse's. (1873)

159

Geology is, perhaps, the simplest and easiest of all physical sciences. It appeals more than any to mere common-sense. It requires fewer difficult experiments, and expensive apparatus. It requires less previous knowledge of other sciences, whether pure or mixed; at least in its rudimentary stages. It is more free from long and puzzling Greek and Latin words. It is, specially, the poor man's science. (1873)

160

I picked up and showed Jowett a chunk of old red sandstone at my feet, flecked with minute white spots, which under my Coddington

Education lens became lichens exquisite in shape and chasing. I recall his almost childlike amazement and delight, his regretful confession that to his mind all natural science was a blank, wisdom at one entrance quite shut out.　(1874)

161

Application for a post as teacher in an infant school
I can teach the following specific subjects paid for as such by the Education Department (Schedule 4, New Code): Mathematics, French, Latin, Physical Geography, Domestic Economy (including Practical Cookery); I can give instruction in Freehand Drawing, Linear Perspective, Model Drawing, Landscape Drawing and Painting in Water Colours; in Needlework and Cutting Out (according to Schedule 3, New Code), in Drill (Calisthenic and Physical Exercises) and in Vocal Music (Old Notation); I also understand the Kindergarten System, the rudiments of German and Italian; and possess a powerful Soprano Voice of more than ordinary compass.　(*c.* 1879)

162

Before leaving Oxford I had arranged to take two reading parties at Toynbee Hall, one in Latin and another in English Literature.... Soon some of the Latin class expressed a wish to learn Greek, so I added a third class....Of the Latin and Greek class the majority were of the lower middle class—but one was a pupil-teacher and one a foreman at the docks. In the Tennyson class I had a journey-man wood-carver.　(1886)

163

At that time there were 216 children belonging to Whitechapel and 344 chargeable to Poplar in the school. The buildings in which they were housed were well-built and commodious, the dining-hall handsome and airy, and the block included an infirmary for the sick, a receiving ward for the newcomers, a laundry and an infant department, all entirely separate from the main building, which consisted chiefly of the school-rooms and the dormitories. These were all lofty and, of course, hideously clean apartments. The children were dressed in a

140

uniform, and no one had his or her own clothes. They wore any that happened to fit, as they were handed out on the day of the weekly change. The soiled garments were sent to the wash, and whether torn or unduly dirty, the delinquent escaped the rebuke or punishment which might have been a training to carefulness. Silence reigned at meal times. The regulation weight of food was handed out to each child according to its age, but regardless of its size, appetite, taste or physical condition....

The hours out of school were not play hours. The girls scrubbed the vast areas, I had almost said acres, of boarded rooms, but they were not allowed to do it together. Each child was placed a few yards off the other. The boys quarrelled or shivered in the yard....

They had no toys, no library, no Sunday School, no places in which to keep personal possessions, no playing fields, no night garments, no prizes, no flowers, no pets, no pictures on the walls, no pleasures in music, no opportunities for seeing the world outside the school walls. Life for them was surrounded with limitations...imposed by an unnatural life and the ruthless requirements of discipline—a discipline which far exceeded what was desirable for the ordering of 10 or 12 children, but which had become necessary because some 600 children had to be considered. (1894)

PEOPLE

164

Among the people whom one must miss out of one's life...by the time one is past fifty, I can only say...that the one I practically and truly miss most next to father and mother...is this Anne, my father's nurse and mine....From her girlhood to her old age, the entire ability of her life was given to serving us. She had a natural gift and speciality for doing disagreeable things; above all, the service of a sick room; so that she was never quite in her glory unless some of us were ill. She had also some parallel speciality for *saying* disagreeable things; and might be relied upon to give the extremely darkest view of any subject, before proceeding to ameliorative action upon it. And she had a very creditable republican aversion to doing immediately and in set terms, as she was bid; so that when my mother and she got old together, and my mother became very imperative and particular about having her teacup set on one side of her little round table, Anne would observantly and punctiliously put it always on the other; which caused my mother to state to me, every morning after breakfast, gravely, that if ever a woman in this world was possessed by the Devil, Anne was that woman. (*c.* 1837)

165

My sister Emily loved the moors. Flowers brighter than the rose bloomed in the blackest of the heath for her; out of a sullen hollow in a livid hillside her mind could make an Eden. She found in the bleak solitude many and dear delights; and not the least and best loved was —liberty. Liberty was the breath of Emily's nostrils; without it she perished. The change from her own home to a school, and from her own very noiseless, very secluded, but unrestricted and unartificial mode of life, to one of disciplined routine...was what she failed in enduring....Every morning, when she woke, the vision of home and the moors rushed on her and darkened and saddened her day.
(*c.* 1837)

Charles [Lear] went as a medical missionary to West Africa. His activities there having been cut short by a serious attack of malaria, he was placed on board ship for England; but at the last moment the captain refused to take him without a nurse. Adjouah, the native girl who had been attending him, immediately offered her services, but Charles, for propriety's sake, ill as he was insisted upon marrying her: so the captain performed the necessary ceremony and they proceeded forthwith to England. On arrival they went to Leatherhead, to Charles's sister Mrs Newsom who... received her brother and his black wife kindly. Adjouah, though her manners, in early Victorian Surrey, were unconventional—she astonished her new relations by pouring the contents of her bedroom jug over her head—was of a lovable nature, and they soon grew very fond of her. She was sent to school for three years, while Charles, recovered from his illness, returned to the mission field, and shortly afterwards died there. Adjouah, her education completed, also became a missionary, and returned to West Africa to work among her own people.   (*c.* 1837)

167

I was taken up a flight of stairs [to the office of Ebenezer Elliott, the Corn Law Rhymer] in Gibraltar Street, and there I found him standing behind the counter. The place was somewhat dingy—fit enough for iron and steel dealing, but scarcely giving one the indication of a poet's study. I was introduced; and though quiet at first, he soon opened up, and, pacing up and down, talked bitterly of 'those dirt-kings—the tax-gorged lords of land'. He was rather slightly formed; his features were somewhat marked by the smallpox; his very shaggy eyebrows overhung his blue eyes; and his head was covered with thick grey hair. The thing uppermost in his mind was 'the Bread Tax'.... 'People think me ferocious', he said, 'but I cannot write gently on that great crime. And yet I could not hurt a fly, even if it stung me.'   (1838)

168

The state of public affairs is not inviting, and I rejoice that we take in no daily paper.   (1839)

Dick Harper—before my time—had been a farm-labourer, but, when I knew him, he had grown old though still hale, was a sort of 'odd man', could assist in loading or unloading a coasting vessel, could act as a scavenger, supply the place of a river bargeman for a day or two, work in a garden....He had mastered the alphabet, and could spell out a word if time were given him....He had a huge fund of good temper and dry humour, and a tolerable stock of stories....He must have been a pretty good actor for, during the Great French War, a press-gang which visited our village carried him off to a ship-of-war, where he played the fool so continually and consistently that he was set on shore, whilst other landsmen no more efficient than he were retained and converted into sailors.

Dick was sincerely religious, and fond of hearing religious books read....'I was working yesterday in Mr R's gardens and 'e was there most part of the day reading. When 'e went away 'e left his book on the seat, and I took en up and look at en. 'Twas called Milton's Paradise Lost. Did 'e ever 'ear tell on?' (*c.* 1840)

170

Mr Hudson is not at all qualified to shine as a speaker....Nature has not fitted him for such displays. He is of extra-aldermanic bulk; his frame is naturally broad and massive, with a tendency to develop every way but upwards. He is scarcely of the middle height, and very rotund; but his chest is broad and well thrown out, and though ungainly, and even clumsy, in his figure and movements, he is strong, active and muscular. He walks with a great effort, his large arms swinging vigorously to aid the difficult action of his legs, yet he gets over the ground more rapidly than the average of men....The more he grows in size...the more active he seems to be. His head is a formidable-looking engine; it is as round and as stern-looking as a forty-two pounder. In fitting it on the body, the formality of a neck has been dispensed with. The face carries a whole battery; the eyes quick and piercing, the mouth firm, a characteristic of resolution. The whole aspect is far removed from the ideal standard of Caucasian beauty, but it is stamped with power....He speaks in volleys, with a thick utterance, as though the voice had to be pumped up from cavernous recesses, and he primes and loads after each discharge. His words are

just those that come first, chiefly monosyllabic, and not always mar-
shalled by the best grammatical discipline; but although he seems to
speak with difficulty, and almost to blunder, yet he succeeds in making
himself thoroughly understood. (1844)

171

Aunt Esther [a clergyman's wife] set herself to subdue me thoroughly.
...I was a very delicate child, and suffered absolute agony from chil-
blains, which were often large open wounds on my feet. Therefore,
I was put to sleep in 'the Barracks'—two dismal unfurnished, uncar-
peted north rooms, without fireplaces, looking into a damp courtyard,
with a well and a howling dog. The only bed was a rough deal trestle,
my only bedding a straw palliasse, with a single coarse blanket. The
only other furniture in the room was a deal chair, and a washing basin
on a tripod. No one was allowed to bring me any hot water; and as the
water in my room always froze with the intense cold, I had to break
the ice with a brass candlestick, or, if that were taken away, with my
wounded hands. If, when I came down in the morning...I was almost
speechless from sickness and misery, it was always declared to be
'temper'. I was given 'saur-kraut' to eat because the very smell of it
made me sick....

I constantly gave [Aunt Esther] the presents which my mother made
me save up all my money to buy for her...but I never spoke to her
unnecessarily. On these occasions I always received a present from
her in return—*The Rudiments of Architecture*, price ninepence, in a red
cover. It was always the same, which not only saved expense, but also
the trouble of thinking. (1845)

172

One day we [Thackeray and his two daughters] had come home from
one of these expeditions in a big blue fly, with a bony horse—it was a
bright blue fly, with a drab inside, and an old white coachman on the
box—my father, after a few words of consultation with the coachman,
drove off again, and shortly afterwards returning on foot, told us he
had just bought the whole concern, brougham and horse and harness, 145

and that he had sent Jackson (our driver had now become Jackson) to be measured for a great-coat. So henceforward we came and went about in our private carriage, which, however, never lost its original name of 'the fly', although Jackson's buttons shone resplendent, with the Thackeray crest, and the horse too seemed brushed up and promoted to be private.   (*c.* 1846)

173

Another of my parishioners was an old man, named William Diplock, who died at Berwick [Sussex] in 1847. He said that if he were a gentleman he would like to travel over England on top of about half a load of hay, drawn by a pair of steady, old oxen.   (1847)

174

[Mrs Alexander] was very tall, serene, and had a beautiful countenance, and her old-fashioned dress was always wonderfully refined and in keeping with her appearance. She seemed to have the power of imposing her own personality upon her surroundings, and subduing the life and movement around her to an intellectual as well as a physical calm. She had a melodious low voice, a delicate Scotch accent, a perfectly self-possessed manner, and a sweet and gentle dignity.... All the clever men who came in contact with her were bound under her spell....

This is one view of Mrs Alexander, and as far as it goes, it is perfectly true....She was also boundlessly subtle, and when she had an object in view she spared no means to attain it. For her own ends, with her sweetness unruffled, she would remorselessly sacrifice her best friends. The most egotistical woman in the world, she *expected* everyone to fall under her spell, and calmly and gently but consistently hated anyone who escaped. Whilst she almost imperceptibly flattered her superiors in rank and position, she ruthlessly and often heartlessly trampled on those whom she...considered her inferiors.
                                                              (1848)

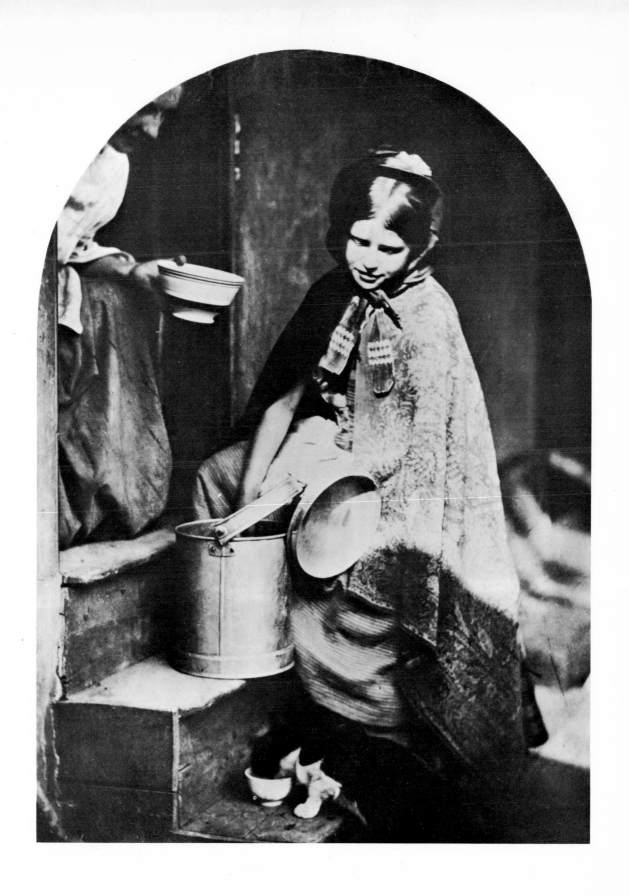

60 '*Feeding the Cat.*' *A photograph by O. G. Rejlander, c. 1857*

61   *Elizabeth Browning, by Field Talfourd, 1859*

62   *John Ruskin, by George Richmond*

63 *Charles Kingsley, by Lowes Dickinson, 1862*

64   *William Morris, by G. F. Watts*

65   *W. E. Gladstone, by Phil May, 1893*

[Walter Savage Landor's] rooms were entirely covered with pictures, the frames fitting close to one another, leaving not the smallest space of wall visible. One or two of these pictures were real works of art, but as a rule he had bought them in Bath, quite willing to believe that the little shops of the Bath dealers could be storehouses of Titians, Giorgiones and Vandycks....Mr Landor lived alone with his beautiful white Spitz dog Pomero, which he allowed to do whatever it liked, and frequently to sit in the oddest way on the bald top of his head. He would talk to Pomero by the hour together, poetry, philosophy, whatever it was he was thinking of, all of it imbued with his own powerful personality, and would often roar with laughter till the whole house seemed to shake....He scarcely ever read, for he only possessed one shelf of books. If anyone gave him a volume, he mastered it and gave it away....He never bought any new clothes and a chimney sweep would have been ashamed to wear his coat, which was always the same so long as I knew him, though it in no way detracted from his majestic and lion-like appearance. (1849)

176

Lord Gage became celebrated in cooking. He wrote and published four works, viz. one on the 'Carpenter's Rule', with its various markings, which to an ordinary person are quite unintelligible; one on 'How to Cook Fish', another on 'The Rubrics'; and the fourth was a new Catechism....

When abroad, on tasting any particular dish which he especially fancied, he would order another like it, and go into the inn kitchen to see it made, and weigh the ingredients with his private scales which he always carried with him. (*c.* 1850)

177

William Sewell...was a man of genuine religious feeling, of real rhetorical and dialectical talent, with an eminent share of the student's practical capacity for acquiring knowledge. On the other hand he had never really mastered any single branch of knowledge, had never been grounded in science and was deficient in the scientific instinct, wanted the sense of humour, and was possessed with a supreme belief in himself. . . . There was a certain taint of insincerity about him—a tendency to be careless of his means provided his purpose was good—which was promptly detected; and his manner which was intended to be winning was too effusive and caressing for the average undergraduate. On the other hand he was respected, as a man who fasted and prayed, and whose fortune and intellect were unreservedly at the service of religion.

(*c.* 1850)

178

Babbage. . . was always worth listening to, but he was a disappointed and discontented man; and his expression was often or generally morose. . . . One day he told me that he had invented a plan by which all fires could be effectively stopped, but added—'I shan't publish it —damn them all, let all their houses be burnt.'. . . Another day he told me that he had seen a pump on a roadside in Italy, with the pious inscription on it to the effect that the owner had erected the pump for the love of God and his country that the tired wayfarer might drink. This led Babbage to examine the pump closely and he soon discovered that every time that a wayfarer pumped some water for himself, he pumped a larger quantity into the owner's house. Babbage then added—'There is only one thing which I hate more than piety, and that is patriotism.'

(*c.* 1850)

179

10 April. At Newmarket on Sunday. . . . It was worth while to be there to see Stanley. A few weeks ago he was on the point of being Prime Minister, which only depended on himself. Then he stood up in the House of Lords, and delivered an oration full of gravity and dignity, such as became the man who had just undertaken to form an Administration. . . . If some grave members of either House of Parliament or any distinguished foreigner who knew nothing of Lord Stanley but what they saw, heard, or read of him, could have suddenly found themselves in the betting room at Newmarket on Tuesday evening and seen Stanley there, I think they would have been in a pretty state of astonishment. There he was in the midst of a crowd of black-legs,

betting men, and loose characters of every description, in uproarious
spirits, chaffing, roaring, and shouting with laughter and joking. His
amusement was to lay Lord Glasgow a wager, that he did not sneeze
in a given time, for which purpose he took pinch after pinch of snuff
while Stanley jeered him or quizzed him with such noise that he drew
the whole mob round him to partake of the coarse merriment he
excited.   (1851)

180

[Rawdon Brown] was one of the kindliest of men...Oxford bred, of
the old-fashioned conservative type, hating modern innovations, loving
the poetry and picturesqueness of the past; solitary in his mode of life,
but of a social disposition, and with a pleasant vein of humour, a wide
range of culture, and quick sympathies that made him a delightful
host. He had come to Venice as a young man, and he spent the last
fifty years of his life there, never, I believe, revisiting England during
all that time. 'I never wake up in the morning but I thank God', he
said, 'that he has let me spend my days in Venice; and sometimes of an
evening, when I go to the Piazzetta, I am afraid to shut my eyes, lest
when I open them I should find it had all been a dream.'   (*c.* 1851)

181

Oh Katie! I wish you could see [Florence Nightingale]....She is tall;
very slight and willowy in figure; thick shortish rich brown hair; very
delicate colouring; grey eyes which are generally pensive and drooping,
but which when they choose can be the merriest eyes I ever saw; and
perfect teeth....Put a long piece of soft net...round this beautifully
shaped head, so as to form a soft white framework for the full oval of
her face (for she had the toothache and so wore this little piece of
drapery) and dress her up in black silk high to the long white round
throat, and a black shawl on and you may get NEAR an idea of her
perfect grace and lovely appearance....She has a great deal of fun, and
is carried along by that, I think. She mimics most capitally; mimics
for instance the way of talking of some of the poor governesses in [her
nursing home], with their delight at having a man servant, and at
having LADY Canning, and LADY Mounteagle to do this and that for
them....She has no friend—and she wants none. She stands perfectly   155

alone half-way between God and his creatures. She used to go a great deal among the villagers here, who dote on her...yet...she will not go among [them] now because her heart and soul are in her hospital plans, and, as she says, she can only attend to one thing at once. She is so excessively gentle in voice, manner, and movement, that one never feels the unbendableness of her character when one is near her. ...She said that if she had influence enough not a mother should bring up a child herself; there should be crèches for the rich as well as the poor. If she had twenty children she would send them all to a crèche, seeing, of course, that it was a well-managed crèche. That exactly tells of what seems to me THE want—but then this want of love for individuals becomes a gift and a very rare one, if one takes it in conjunction with her intense love for the RACE; her utter unselfishness in serving and ministering. (1854)

182

Mrs Browning...is very small, not more than 4 feet 8 inches I should think. She is brown, with dark eyes and dead brown hair, and she has white teeth and a low harsh voice, her eyes are bright and full of life, she has a manner full of charm and kindness. She rarely laughs, but is always cheerful and smiling. She is great upon mysticism and listens with a solemn eager manner to any nonsense people like to tell her upon that subject. Her husband is not unlike her. (c. 1855)

183

My mother's face was finely formed, with straight brows and dark hair and eyelashes over blue-grey eyes; these, with the long, delicately shaped aquiline nose, were lovely. Her long white throat and graceful bearing made her look taller than she really was. She possessed a most characteristic love of beautiful things. She looked upon it as a duty to make herself and everything round her as perfect as possible. Her dress, for instance, was always of the best materials, and she insisted on having it sewn with silk on both sides; when we asked her, irreverently, what difference it could make whether they were sewn with silk or cotton, she would reply, 'I should know that it was cotton and should not like that'. She made all her own close caps of Honiton lace, with lappets to her shoulders, because the fashionable shapes were neither tasteful nor simple enough. She loved to be surrounded with flowers, but they were all carefully chosen for their sweetness and colouring (she disliked yellow flowers); ordinary garden flowers gave her no especial pleasure, and even as little children we only offered her roses out of our gardens, or bunches of scented geranium leaves, lemon verbena, or mignonette. She kept a little bottle of attar of roses in her workbox, and her rooms had an indefinable fragrance of lavender and violets about them.... Bottled scents were far too coarse for her, and if she suspected musk to be in them they were sent away at once. Her wrath at being subjected to such smells as gas, coal-smoke, or lamp-oil, etc., was strong and despairing; and no member of her large household ventured to strike a match or blow out a candle, in any room into which she was likely to come within half an hour after the rash act. If possible she would never *touch* a penny and if it could not be avoided, hurried to wash her hands; she always washed the silver or gold coins before giving them in the offertory.... During the first year of her married life she managed not to call her husband anything and as soon as Alice [her first child] could speak adopted the child's name for him, addressing him as 'Papa' from that time forward. I remember perfectly when they had been married more than twenty years, hearing him coax her to call him by his name; he refused to give up a charming cloak he had bought for her until it was said. After a long time, and with the greatest difficulty she whispered, 'Thank you, George', but it was never said again.

(*c.* 1860)

184

25 December. Married a young parishioner of the name of Mahershallalashbaz Tuck. He accounted for the possession of so extraordinary a name thus: his father wished to call him by the shortest name in the Bible, and for that purpose selected Uz. But, the clergyman making some demur, the father said in pique, 'Well, if he cannot have the shortest he shall have the longest'.

(1866)

185

Just where the lane hedges and enclosures began [on the Welsh–Herefordshire border] we met a humble cavalcade coming up the mountain. There was an old basket-maker leading a small bay pony,

People poor and thin, with a good deal of its hair rubbed off and loaded with the implements and materials of the trade. The old man led by the other hand a small stout rosy-cheeked girl with dark eyes, she holding a chubby child upon a donkey. The old man said he was going to Talgarth, but he lived in Gloucestershire where he had eleven at home. Not catching what he had said and thinking he was speaking of his beasts I asked if he were saying he had eleven donkeys at home. So he smiled and said 'Short-eared ones, eleven children'. He was a quaint humorous old fellow and we chaffed him about having shaved the rubbed hairless place on the pony to see what colour the pony was underneath.... These wandering people seem to find a strange fascination in the wild free kind of life and after they have once taken to gypsying seldom care to settle down again. Regular work becomes irksome to them.   (1870)

186

The figure of the lecturer was striking, with ample gown—discarded often when its folds became too hopelessly involved—and the velvet college cap.... The quaintness of his costume—the light home-spun tweed, the double-breasted waistcoat, the ill-fitting and old-fashioned frock-coat, the amplitude of the inevitable blue tie—accurately reflected something of the originality of his mind and talk. If it were not for the peculiarly delicate hands and tapering fingers...the Oxford professor might have been taken for an old-fashioned country gentleman. In repose his face was at this time furrowed into sadness; but the blue eyes, piercing from beneath thick bushy eyebrows, never ceased to shine with the fire of genius; whilst the smile that was never long absent when he lectured, lit up his face with the radiance of a singularly gracious and gentle spirit. His voice, though not very strong, had a peculiar *timbre*, which was at once penetrating and attractive. His old-fashioned pronunciation, with the peculiar roll of the r's, seemed in perfect harmony with the mediaeval strain in his thought.
                                                    (*c.* 1883)

187

He used to sit in a subdued fury of impatience, waiting till everyone was settled down, and if the noise of settling down went on a moment after he had hoped it was over, there was an agony, shown only by his

martyred face and in the drumming of his pencil on the desk. Then in <inline type="marginalia">*People*</inline>
the silence the high rich shrillness of his voice came streaming out
under the closed eyelids in his ivory face. We are not likely to see anything more resembling the phenomenon of inspiration. I find my
mental picture has completed itself with curls of pale blue smoke from
a tripod. (1892)

188

What will strike him most, perhaps, in the Oxford of today, is the dis-
appearance of the Don. Oxford is Young Oxford. The queer figures,
strange compounds of shyness and hauteur, who formed the still background to all the movement and variety of academical life, have faded
away into quiet parsonages. With them Oxford has lost its last relic
of continuity....It has not lost sweetness in them or light, but it
certainly has lost individuality. They were not as other men are. They
had in fact a deep quiet contempt for other men. Oxford was their
world, and beyond Oxford lay only waste wide regions of shallowness
and inaccuracy. They were often men of keen humour, of humour keen
enough at any rate to see and to mock at the mere presence of 'the
world of progress' around them....Their delight was to take a 'pro-
gressive idea' and to roast it over the common-room fire. They had
their poetry; for the place itself, and the reverence they felt for it, filled
them with a quiet sense of the beautiful; and this refinement and this
humour both saved them from bowing before the vulgar gods of the
world without. They did not care much for money; they saw their
contemporaries struggling for it, and lingered on content with their
quiet rooms and four hundred a year. They cared very little for fame
...although most of them had a great dreamwork on hand, of which
not a chapter was ever written. What they did care for was strangely
blended of the venerable and the ridiculous, for their real love of
learning was mingled with a pedantry both of mind and of life, and a
feminine rigour over the little observances of society and discipline.
Such as they were, however, Young Oxford has no type of existence
to show so picturesque, so individual. (1901)

THE HOME

66 *Scarisbrick Hall, Lancashire. The south front with Pugin's Great Hall in the centre*

Victorian architecture was dominated by 'the Battle of the Styles', between a romantic neo-Gothic that stood for a revived religion and a renewed chivalry, and a heavy late-Georgian classicism that stood for the established order. The best known example of the first in London is the Houses of Parliament, designed by Barry in 1841; that of the second is the handsome terraced residences of the Victorian residential developments of Kensington and Bayswater, with their symmetrical stuccoed fronts and their pillared front doors raised above an area. Every city of any size has its equivalent architectures, the Gothic often represented by a town hall and some handsome churches, elaborately fitted, in new residential districts of houses in both styles.

New materials were chiefly used in the Gothic style. Cast iron, which Repton had employed as early as 1800, was combined with glass in J. D. Bunning's London Coal Exchange of 1849, to create a splendid domed inner court, roofed in glass; it has recently been destroyed by officialdom. The style was popularized and cheapened in Paxton's Crystal Palace of 1850–51, destroyed by Hitler in the last war.

These characteristic Victorian creations are all urban, for the men whose increased wealth demanded new quarters naturally congregated in the towns where their money was made. Urban, too, were the mean houses, sometimes in the north back-to-back, that were built for the families who came to the towns to work in the factories.

The comparatively few great country houses, and the much larger number of suburban villas, erected in the Victorian age, all keep a rather urban look, and seem more like extensions of the town than homes that belong to the country. One man had the house, Owlpen Manor, that he built in the depths of Gloucestershire, designed on the model of his London club.

Most of us have known Victorian interiors; their solidity and comfort have ensured their survival. We remember their innumerable pictures and the bibelots on whatnots and chiffoniers. We are apt to think of them in terms of the pre-Raphaelites (who first made their public appearance in 1845), of John Ruskin, William Morris, Whistler, and the Tottenham Court Road. In fact the pre-Raphaelites and Ruskin were completely uninterested in interior decoration; Whistler was an American painter working for a small London clique; and all that mattered were William Morris and the Tottenham Court Road. It was a Battle of the Styles on a wider front.

The aristocratic houses were so magnificently endowed from the Georgian era that most of them needed no change beyond greater comfort in the bedrooms, of a kind easily bought in the Tottenham Court Road; only a few, such as Naworth, acquired splendid and expensive 'artistic' carpets and curtains from Morris and Co. The upper middle classes had no such patrimony and were thankful for the artistic productions of Morris, and for the commercial comfort provided by Mr Maple.

Comfort, indeed, in domestic furnishing, was a Victorian discovery and it ultimately became more important than the Georgian notion of elegance. Chairs and sofas were stuffed and padded as never before, curtains were wadded, carpets (now machine-made) were wide if rarely thick. Yet these comforts were modified by the curious masochistic tradition of the public schools: beds *had* to be hard and stuffed with horsehair; baths *had* to be cold; and any interest in decoration was 'soft', feminine and despicable.

12

The Home   The true middle classes were perfectly happy with the commercial production that culminated in the 1851 exhibition, though fortunately for their descendants they preserved, out of family feeling, most of their ancestral furniture; and the 'lower classes' only asked for tables and chairs and cupboards and beds with which they could live. Yet many country farmhouses of a modest sort preserved for appreciative descendants an eighteenth-century chair or two, and perhaps even an earlier chest. In contrast, the Irish immigrants had already discovered how to live with packing cases.

The invention of photography had brought a new criterion into every form of art: naturalism. Henry Fox Talbot's publication of his Calotypes—'the Pencil of Nature'—in 1844–45 made people conscious of what things looked like without the creative intervention of the artist. In the next few years photographic studios were opened in London and the work of all but the most skilful and flattering portraitists was at an end. By 1857, photographs of the Derby were taken on the course for W. P. Frith, to be used by him in the portrayal of the crowd in his famous *Derby Day*—the Academy picture of the year in 1858.

This same interest in naturalism was reflected in decorative art. Everything was patterned—wallpapers, chintzes, floor-coverings—and nearly every pattern was brightly floral in a naturalistic style. The same style was extended to work in the round in the most appreciated exhibits at the 1851 exhibition. It was only Morris who wanted to stylize Nature in an archaizing way.

67   *'Orchard' tapestry, designed by William Morris, 1890.*

William Morris drew his inspiration from the handicrafts of the *The Home* Middle Ages; but he liked Queen Anne furniture, and, for his wall-papers, owed more than is realized to seventeenth-century France. He brought lofty and uncommercial ideals into decoration, and though little of his furniture was successful, his gift for design made his textiles and wallpapers delightful. He was one of the creators and leaders of English socialism; yet his decorative productions were characteristic of the houses of the upper middle class. His aphorism is still valid: 'Have nothing in your houses that you do not know to be useful or believe to be beautiful.'

189

The principal thing worthy of observation in the lowland cottage of England is its finished neatness. The thatch is firmly pegged down, and mathematically levelled at the edges; and, though the martin is permitted to attach his humble domicile, in undisturbed security, to the eaves, he may be considered as enhancing the effect of the cottage, by increasing its usefulness, and making it contribute to the comfort of more beings than one. The whitewash is stainless, and its rough surface catches a side light as brightly as a front one; the luxuriant rose is trained gracefully over the window; and the gleaming lattice, divided not into heavy squares, but into small pointed diamonds, is thrown half open, as is just discovered by its glance among the green leaves of the sweet briar, to admit the breeze, that, as it passes over the flowers, becomes full of their fragrance. The light wooden porch breaks the flat of the cottage face by its projection; and a branch or two of wandering honeysuckle spread over the low hatch. A few square feet of garden, and a latched wicket, persuading the weary and dusty pedestrian, with expressive eloquence, to lean upon it for an instant, and request a drink of water or milk, complete a picture, which, if it be far enough from London to be unspoiled by town sophistications, is a very perfect thing in its way. The ideas it awakens are agreeable, and the architecture is all that we want in such a situation. It is pretty and appropriate; and if it boasted of any other perfection, it would be at the expense of its propriety. (1837–38)   163

Almost all we are obliged to read, or see, or hear, or handle, all the present productions mental or manual of British toil have a Brummagem stamp about them—books, pictures, statues, edifices, no less than cast-iron ware and cutlery—almost all articles from minikin pins up to new parish churches, from encyclopedias down to children's alphabets, are Brummagem, essentially Brummagem—undertaken by contract, executed per order, put forth in the gross, and paid for in the lump, showy and perishable, promising to do more than they need, accomplishing little that they ought, satisfied with the minimum of merit which shall ensure them a market.   (1840)

191

Every great town has one or more slums, where the working class is crowded together. True, poverty often dwells in hidden alleys close to the palaces of the rich; but, in general, a separate territory has been assigned to it, where, removed from the sight of the happier classes, it may struggle along as it can. These slums are pretty equally arranged in all the great towns of England, the worst houses in the worst quarters of the towns; usually one- or two-storied cottages in long rows, perhaps with cellars used as dwellings, almost always irregularly built, unpaved, rough, dirty, filled with vegetable and animal refuse, without sewers or gutters, but supplied with foul stagnant pools instead. . . . Further, the streets serve as drying-grounds in fine weather; lines are stretched across from house to house, and hung with wet clothing.
                         (1844)

192

The most horrible spot. . .lies on the Manchester side, immediately south-west of Oxford Road, and is known as Little Ireland. In a rather deep hole, in a curve of the Medlock and surrounded on all four sides by tall factories and high embankments, covered with buildings, stand two groups of about two hundred cottages, built chiefly back to back, in which live about 4000 human beings, most of them Irish. The cottages are old, dirty, and of the smallest sort, the streets uneven, fallen into ruts and in part without drains or pavements. Masses of

refuse, offal and sickening filth lie among standing pools in all direc-
tions; the atmosphere is poisoned by the effluvia from these, and laden
and darkened by the smoke of a dozen tall factory chimneys. A horde
of ragged women and children swarm about here, as filthy as the swine
that feed upon the garbage heaps and in the puddles.... In each of
these pens, containing at most two rooms, a garret and perhaps a
cellar, on the average twenty human beings live. (1844)

68 *'Over London by Rail', by Gustave Doré*

Architectural Decoration

Mr J. Chase, having devoted much study to the Architecture and Decoration of the times of Henry VII, Francis I, Elizabeth, etc., down to the life of Louis XIV, respectfully announces he is prepared to execute all works he may be honoured with, with strict fidelity to the period proposed to be illustrated.   (1844)

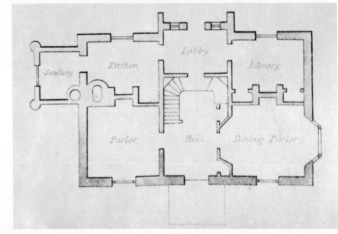

69   *Elevation and plan for a small house in the Tudor style*

One of the first things I can remember when we came to London is the old house in Cheyne Row, the home of Mr and Mrs Carlyle. Its stillness, its dimness, its panelled walls, its carved banisters, and the quiet garden behind, where at intervals in the brickwork lay the tobacco pipes all ready for use....

In the dining-room stood that enchanting screen, covered with pictures, drawings, prints, fashions, portraits without end, which my father liked so much; upstairs was the panelled drawing-room with its windows to the Row, and the portrait of Oliver Cromwell hanging opposite the windows. But best of all, there was Mrs Carlyle herself, a living picture...slim, bright, dark-eyed, upright, in her place.... She used to be handsomely dressed in velvet and point lace. She sat there at leisure, and prepared for conversation. She was not familiar, but cordial, dignified, and interested in everything, as she sat installed in her corner of the sofa by one of the little tables covered with nickknacks of silver and mother-of-pearl.

(1846)

195

Hence then a general law, of singular importance in the present day, a law of simple common-sense—not to decorate things belonging to purposes of active and occupied life. Wherever you can rest, there decorate; where rest is forbidden, so is beauty. You must not mix ornament with business, any more than you may mix play. Work first, and then rest. Work first, and then gaze, but do not use golden ploughshares, nor bind ledgers in enamel. Do not thrash with sculptured flails; nor put bas-reliefs on millstones. What! it will be asked, are we in the habit of doing so? Even so; always and everywhere. The most familiar position of Greek mouldings is in these days on shop fronts. There is not a tradesman's sign nor shelf nor counter in all the streets of all our cities, which has not upon it ornaments which were invented to adorn temples and beautify kings' palaces. There is not the smallest advantage in them where they are. Absolutely valueless—utterly without the power of giving pleasure, they only satiate the eye, and vulgarize their own forms. Many of these are in themselves thoroughly good copies of fine things, which things themselves we shall never, in consequence, enjoy any more. Many a pretty beading and graceful bracket there is in wood or stucco above our grocers' and cheesemongers' and hosiers' shops: how is it that the tradesmen cannot understand that custom is to be had only by selling good tea and cheese and cloth, and that people come to them for their honesty, and their readiness, and their right wares, and not because they have Greek cornices over their windows, or their names in large gilt letters on their house fronts? How pleasure-able it would be to have the power of going through the streets of London, pulling down those brackets and friezes and large names, re-storing to the tradesmen the capital they had spent in architecture, and putting them on honest and equal terms, each with his name in black letters over his door, not shouted down the street from the upper storeys, and each with a plain wooden shop casement, with small panes in it that people would not think of breaking in order to be sent to prison! How much better for them would it be—how much happier, how much wiser, to put their trust upon their own truth and industry, and not on the idiocy of their customers. It is curious, and it says little for our national probity on the one hand, or prudence on the other, to see the whole system of our street decoration based on the idea that people must be baited to a shop as moths are to a candle.   (1848)

196

[Of imitations in gutta percha, putty, plaster, carton pierre, etc.] The great cheapness of the substitute, compared with the real material, in-evitably leads to excess. Such ornament always seems added or applied, stuck on as it were, and can rarely be made to appear as a part of con-struction.   (1851)

197

It is impossible to examine the works of the Great Exhibition without seeing how often utility and construction are made secondary to dec-oration. In fact, when commencing a design, designers are too apt to think of ornament before construction and...rather to construct orna-ment than to ornament construction. This, on the slightest examina-tion, will be found to be the leading error in the exhibition, an error... which is apt to sicken us of decoration, and lead us to admire those objects of utility (the machines and utensils of various kinds) where use is so paramount that ornament is repudiated, and, fitness of pur-pose being the end sought, a noble simplicity is the result.   (1851)

70   *Exhibits at the Great Exhibition in the Crystal Palace, from the*
Art Journal Illustrated Catalogue, 1851.

71 *The Saloon at Highclere Castle, decorated by Thomas Allom, c. 1862*

72 'Allanbank', a house in Camden Road, London, designed by
Henry Hodge, 1863

73 *The entrance front at Waddesdon Manor, Buckinghamshire. The house was designed for Baron Ferdinand de Rothschild by G. H. Destailleur in 1874*

74 *Bronze ornament, by San Giovanni, exhibited at the Great Exhibition,
from the Art Journal Illustrated Catalogue, 1851*

75 *'Renaissance' sideboard exhibited by T. W. Caldecott at the Great
Exhibition, from the Art Journal Illustrated Catalogue, 1851*

A magnificent centre ornament and *plateau* by Messrs Hunt and Roskell....It is adapted as a stand for flowers by day, and as a candelabrum by night; and with these objects the various groups are selected to agree in subject. On each quarter of the *plateau* are groups representing the seasons: Flora, attended by her nymphs, playing with flowers and a lamb, personifying Spring; Zephyrs, bearing on their shoulders a female figure crowned with wheat, and carrying the sickle, representing Summer. Autumn is typified by the figures of Silenus, Bacchus and Pomona; Winter by aged Saturnus, who, seated on a leafless tree, spreads his mantle over shivering nature. On his left is a figure representing storm and tempest, accompanied by wolves. Beneath the groups are the signs of the Zodiac. On the foot of the centre ornament are figures representing the quarters of the world, each being accompanied by appropriate animals. The *alto relievo* around the column represents Day and Night, attended by the Hours; around the stem which supports the vase are four figures, representing the elements. The whole is richly decorated with ornament of the *Cinque Cento* period.   (1851)

199

I think one of the chief delights was the white dimity curtains in the bedrooms, they in their first freshness always contained a good deal of the essence of the first evening in the country, when we children roamed from room to room...and then out again to the garden wild with happiness and resting in the knowledge that it was to last a whole summer.   (1852)

200

You will all admit that there is neither romance nor comfort in waiting at your own or at any one else's door on a windy and rainy day, till the servant comes from the end of the house to open it. You all know the critical nature of that opening—the drift of wind into the passage, the impossibility of putting down the umbrella at the proper moment without getting a cupful of water dropped down the back of your neck from the top of the doorway; and you know how little these inconveniences are abated by the common Greek portico at the top of the steps. You know how the east winds blow through those unlucky couples of pillars, which are all that your architects find consistent with due observance of the Doric order. Then, away with these absurdities; and the next house you build, insist upon having the pure old Gothic porch, walled in on both sides, with its pointed arch entrance and gabled roof above. Under that, you can put down your umbrella at your leisure, and, if you will, stop a moment to talk with your friend as you give him the parting shake of the hand. And if now and then a wayfarer found a moment's rest on a stone seat on each side of it, I believe you would find the insides of your houses not one whit the less comfortable; and, if you answer me, that were such refuges built in the open streets, they would become mere nests of filthy vagrants, I reply that I do not despair of such a change in the administration of the poor laws of this country, as shall no longer leave any of our fellow-creatures in a state in which they would pollute the steps of our houses by resting upon them for a night. (1853)

201

It is evident to the stranger that as the gable-ended houses, which obtrude themselves corner-wise on the widening street, fall vacant, they are pulled down to allow greater space for traffic and a more modern style of architecture. The quaint and narrow shop-windows of fifty years ago are giving way to large panes and plate-glass. Nearly every dwelling seems devoted to some branch of commerce. In passing hastily through the town, one hardly perceives where the necessary doctor and lawyer can live, so little appearance is there of any dwellings of the professional middle class.... Grey stone abounds, and the rows of houses built of it have a kind of solid grandeur connected with their uniform and enduring lines. The framework of the doors and the lintels of the windows, even in the smallest dwellings, are made of blocks of stone. There is no painted wood to require continual beautifying, or else a shabby aspect; and the stone is kept scrupulously clean by the notable Yorkshire housewives. (1857)

202

Another great evil in house construction is carrying drains underneath the house. Such drains are never safe.... How few there are who can intelligently trace disease, in their households, to such causes! Is it not a fact, that when scarlet fever, measles, or small-pox appear among

the children, the very first thought which occurs is 'where' the child
can have 'caught' the disease? And the parents immediately run over
in their minds all the families with whom they may have been. They
never think of looking at home for the source of the mischief.

(1860)

203

The anniversary of [The Ladies' Sanitary] association was held yesterday
at the Hanover Square Rooms. The Bishop of Oxford, who presided, ad-
vocated the claims of the association upon the several grounds of religion,
humanity and self-interest, showing the effect of its operations in making
it possible for the poor to become religious and respectable, reducing the
amount of disease and death, and lowering the taxation of the country.
The association did this in the most direct manner by teaching the
poor to help themselves, and the promotion of such objects had a
tendency to lessen the separation which gradually grew up between
the rich and the poor and between different classes of religionists, in
proportion to the increase of wealth and of the intensity of Christian
principle. Mr Thomas Hughes, author of *Tom Brown's Schooldays*,
proposed the first resolution, which was seconded by Dr Lankester,
who dwelt with considerable warmth upon the duty of lessening the
mortality of the population by disseminating information as to the
laws of life and health, a knowledge of which, he considered, should not
by a false delicacy be withheld from females, for it was their ignorance
of the subject that caused a vast number of deaths, which could as
easily be prevented as deaths from accidents upon railways....

The Bishop of London said there was, no doubt, a great want of
sanitary knowledge, but there was a greater want of sanitary belief;
the poor needed the importance of cleanliness to be brought home to
them; and if they were saved from an epidemic, for instance, by means
of the brushes and whitewash which he was glad to find the missionaries
of the association carried with them, they would see there was something practical in what was told them by the lecturer.   (1861)

204

Across the street [in Whitchurch]...is a chemist's shop, which is also
a post office....The two storeys are rather lower than one of an average
London house, so that we will hope the folks inside are not tall; but
there is a grand peaked roof with dormers, in which I suppose servants

The Home are tucked away. But I hold my nose at the thought. In the window are a dozen bottles—some near a hundred years old, with drugs of ditto age. One hopes they are all labelled right. The only one I can answer for is one of poppy heads, so I suppose toothaches are known here. There are also two plaster of Paris horses, indicating that horse-balls may be had within; a case of scents; an accordion; two framed prints—one seemingly of a military, the other of a fox-hunting nature, evidently by a French artist; a bottle or two filled with what looks humiliatingly like lollipops; and a blue tablet bearing a golden inscription....In front, instead of pavement, are great flints and a row of posts, which prevent the carriages of Whitchurch from rushing into the house windows, and the drunken men thereof from losing their way home. There are also two gutters, down which are running now gallons, ay, tons, of true London milk—chalk and water, with a slight tinge of animal matter....There was a Methodist parson walked up to the station an hour ago;...and there was a shepherd came and stood in the exact centre of the town, of course with an umbrella (all Chalk shepherds have umbrellas) and has been doing nothing certainly for an hour, in pouring rain. Also a groom boy went by, who looked as if he had been expelled from Lord Portsmouth's stables for dirt. And there you have the Whitchurch news. (1863)

205

Smoking-Room

The pitiable resources to which some gentlemen are driven, even in their own houses, in order to be able to enjoy the pestiferous luxury of a cigar, have given rise to the occasional introduction of an apartment specially dedicated to the use of Tobacco. The Billiard-room is sometimes allowed to be more or less under the dominion of the smoker, if contrived accordingly; but this would in other cases be impossible; and there are even instances where, out of sheer encouragement of the practice, a retreat is provided altogether apart, where the *dolce far niente* in this particular shape may solely and undisturbedly reign.

(1864)

206

Housekeeper's Room

This is primarily the Business-room and Parlour of the housekeeper. The fittings, besides the ordinary furniture of a plain Sitting-room,

178

will consist of spacious presses, from 18 to 24 inches deep, filled with
drawers and shelving, for the accommodation of preserves, pickles,
fancy groceries of all kinds, cakes, china, glass, linen and so forth. It
may be worth while to note that sugar is kept in drawers or canisters;
tea in canisters; spiceries and light groceries in small drawers; cakes
and biscuits in canisters. . . .

The upper servants take breakfast and tea, and perhaps pass the
evening, with the housekeeper in this room. . . . The same persons dine
here also if there be no steward's room. (1864)

207

Bath-room

No house of any pretensions will be devoid of a general Bath-room;
and in a large house there must be several of these. The sort of apartment usually required is simply one that shall be large enough to con-
tain a reclining-bath and a fireplace, with perhaps a shower-bath
either separate or over the other, and sufficient space for dressing. If
there be hot-water apparatus of any sort in the house, the bath-rooms
ought to be placed with special reference to a supply. . . . Cold water of
course must be supplied, and a waste-pipe laid to the drain. (1864)

208

[The author] recommends grey paper for the drawing-room, with
inscriptions from the book of Job such as 'Man is born unto travail as
the sparks fly upward' painted in black letters in diagonal lines.

(*c.* 1870)

209

Anyone who knows what the worth of family affection is among the
lower classes and who has seen the array of little portraits stuck over a
labourer's fireplace, still gathering into one the 'Home' that life is
always parting—the boy that has 'gone to Canada', the girl 'out at
service', the little one. . . that sleeps under the daisies, the old grandfather in the country—will perhaps feel with me that in counteracting
the tendencies, social and industrial, which every day are sapping the
healthier family affections, the 6*d.* photograph is doing more for the
poor than all the philanthropists in the world. (1871) 179

76   *Bedford Park, London. A group of houses in a middle-class*
residential area, c. 1880

77   *Mabel Love's Drawing-room, c. 1890*

78   *Lily Langtry's bedroom, c. 1896*

The most formidable obstacle which lies in the way of any attempt to reform the arts of design in this country, is perhaps the indifference with which people of even reputed taste are accustomed to regard the products of common industry. (1873)

211

The school-room was high and narrow, with a very old carpet, and a very old piano, some books, two globes, and a good deal of feminine rubbish in the way of old work-baskets, unfinished sewing, etc. There were two long windows, the lower halves of which were covered with paint. This mattered the less as the only view from them was of back-yards, roofs and chimneys. (1873)

212

Beauty had existed long before 1880. It was Mr Oscar Wilde who managed her début. To study the period is to admit that to him was due no small part of the social vogue that Beauty began to enjoy. Fired by his fervid words men and women hurled their mahogany into the streets and ransacked the curio-shops for the furniture of Annish days. Dados grew upon every wall, sunflowers and the feathers of peacocks curved in every corner. Tea grew quite cold while the guests were praising the Willow Pattern of its cup. A few fashionable women even dressed themselves in sinuous draperies and unheard-of greens. Into whatsoever ballroom you went, you would surely find, among the women in tiaras and the fops and the distinguished foreigners, half a score of comely ragamuffins in velveteen, murmuring sonnets, posturing, waving their hands. (1880)

213

A room is like a picture.... The main point of interest to which the decorations should work up, is the inhabitants; but as they can never be reckoned upon, the picture must be composed as it were without the subject, like a poem without a point or a story without an end. This must be done by keeping the tone of colour down. (1881)

I've been in most Casual Wards in London; was in the one in Macklin Street, Drury Lane, last week. They keep you two nights and a day, and more than that if they recognize you. You have to break 10 cwt. of stone, or pick 4 lb. of oakum. Both are hard. About thirty a night go to Macklin Street. The food is 1 pint of gruel and 6 oz. bread for breakfast, 8 oz. bread and 1½ oz. cheese for dinner; tea same as breakfast. No supper. It is not enough to do the work on. Then you are obliged to bathe, of course; sometimes three will bathe in one water, and if you complain they turn nasty, and ask if you are come to a palace.   (1890)

215

[York Cottage, Sandringham] was...a glum little villa, encompassed by thickets of laurel and rhododendron, shadowed by huge Wellingtonias and separated by an abrupt run of lawn from a pond, at the edge of which a leaden pelican gazes in dejection upon the water lilies and bamboos. The local brown stone in which the house is constructed is concealed by rough-cast which in its turn is enlivened by very imitation Tudor beams....The Duke's own sitting room, its north window blocked by heavy shrubberies, was rendered even darker by the red cloth-covering which saddened the walls. Against this dismal monochrome (which was composed of the cloth used in those days for the trousers of the French Army) hung excellent reproductions of some of the more popular pictures acquired by the Chantrey Bequest.

(1892)

TRANSPORT AND TRADE

79 *The Port of London, 1842*

Victorian England rose on the tide of commercial prosperity that had begun to flow nearly seventy years before. Yet the tide flowed over rocks and quicksands.

The Factory Act of 1825, which only concerned cotton mills, had prescribed that no person was to work in the mills for more than twelve hours a day, exclusive of an hour and a half for meal times, with nine hours on Saturdays. The next act, that of 1833, extended to all textile mills except those making lace. It prohibited work between 8.30 p.m. and 5.30 a.m., and enacted that no one under eighteen was to work more than twelve hours a day or sixty-nine hours a week. Within three years from the passing of the act, no child under thirteen was to work more than forty-eight hours a week, or more than nine hours in any one day. Factory inspectors were appointed to see that these regulations were respected.

In the early years of Victoria's reign, from 1841 to 1847, factory legislation was centred upon the employment of women. There were so many women in the mills that there was some fear that they might displace men operatives, and there was an attempt to establish a ratio and to prohibit married women from work. In 1844 an act was nearly passed restricting women and children to a ten-hour day; but the House changed its mind at the last minute, and it was only in 1847–48, a year of slump, that the Ten Hours Bill for women and children between thirteen and eighteen became law.

These acts only concerned textile workers, but other trades were gradually included. In 1843 the Royal Commission on Mines investigated the conditions under which women and children worked underground, and as a result their labour was prohibited. In 1860 the Factory Acts were extended to include calico printers, bleachers and dyers, and in the following years, the workers at machine-made lace. In 1864 all sorts of non-textile factories came under regulation and in 1867 a more general act covered most industrial enterprises. It was not until 1881 that the employer's liability for accidents caused by his negligence, or that of his foreman, was legally recognized.

These restrictive regulations were made against a background of a vast increase in manufacture. That increase took place against a background of total change in transport. In 1838 the first steamer—the *Great Eastern*—a wooden ship 235 feet long, powered by an engine of 400 h.p.—began to sail from Liverpool to New York. She reckoned to take fifteen days from Liverpool and thirteen in the reverse direction. In 1845 the *Great Britain* steamship of Bristol, designed by Sir Isambard Brunel, was launched—322 feet long, of 2984 tons displacement. It was no faster than the *Great Eastern*—it reached New York in just under fifteen days from Liverpool—but it was made of iron and driven by a screw. Yet even in 1858 the ratio of sail to steam at sea was still about forty-five to one.

Even before Queen Victoria's accession railways had begun to function in Britain, with steam locomotives. The Stockton and Darlington Line had been opened in 1825, the Liverpool and Manchester in 1830.

In 1838 the London and Birmingham Railway, the work of Robert Stephenson, was opened. Three years later the London and Brighton 185

Leeds from Holbeck Junction, 1868

Railway was opened, and the Great Western all the way to Bristol—the longest railway, $117\frac{1}{2}$ miles, that then existed.

The progress of railways was not merely an adventure in transport, but also a speculation on an unexampled scale. Nearly 44 million new railway shares were issued in 1845; 132 million in 1846. The splendid Shareholders' Hall and the classical gateway of Euston remained until 1963 to show that the Railway Companies had a sense of dignity; and the fact that any traveller from Paddington sees Frith's *Railway Station* with a pleasurable shock of recognition shows that they could build for the future.

The other great change in communication was the institution of the penny post. In London a 2*d.* post had functioned since 1801 with what now seems fantastic speed; outside the Metropolis there were extraordinary variations in time and expense. The amount due had to be ascertained and marked on every packet; postmasters had to keep elaborate accounts and be debited with any unpaid postage; and all letters had to be paid for by the recipient. It cost 8*d.* to send a single sheet of paper weighing less than an ounce from London to Brighton.

In 1837 Rowland Hill published a pamphlet, entitled *Post Office Reform*, that pointed out that over the past twenty years the population of Great Britain had increased by some 6 million, but that the postal revenues had slightly diminished. He recommended a flat rate of 1*d.* for each $\frac{1}{2}$ oz. for letters posted and delivered in the United Kingdom, with excess for heavier packets, and maintained that the increase of correspondence would more than cover the cost. In 1839 the Budget proposed a uniform penny postage, and a fresh web of communication was established to supplement that of the railways.

I...got upon the railroad [at Birmingham] at 7.30. Nothing can be more comfortable than the vehicle in which I was put, a sort of chariot with two places, and there is nothing disagreeable about it but the occasional whiffs of stinking air which it is impossible to exclude altogether. The first sensation is a slight degree of nervousness and a feeling of being run away with, but a sense of security soon supervenes and the velocity is delightful. Town after town, one park and château after another, are left behind with the rapid variety of a moving panorama, and the continual bustle and animation of the changes and stoppages make the journey very entertaining. (1837)

217

In 1837–38 I was living near Leighton Buzzard while the London and Birmingham Railway...was in process of construction and when the first section was opened to Watford, I travelled by it to London, third class, in what is now an ordinary goods truck, with neither roof nor seats nor any other accommodation than is now given to coal, iron, and miscellaneous goods. If it rained, or the wind was cold, the passengers sat on the floor and protected themselves as they could. Second-class carriages were then what the very worst of the third class are or were a few years ago—closed in, but low and nearly dark, with plain, wooden seats—while the first class were exactly like the bodies of three stage-coaches joined together. (1837–38)

218

The London and Birmingham Railway having been completed in September 1838, after being about five years in progress, the great main system of railway communication between London, Liverpool, and Manchester was then opened to the public.... It was already amusing to hear the complaints of the travellers about the slowness of the coaches as compared with the railway, though the coaches travelled at a speed of eleven miles an hour. (1838)

It is not too much to say that without Nasmyth's steam-hammer
[invented 1829] we must have stopped short in many of those gigantic
engineering works which, but for the decay of all wonder in us, would
be the perpetual wonder of this age.... The manufacture of large
articles in *dies* [makes it possible for railway wheels to be] manu-
factured with enormous economy.... The various parts of the wheels
are produced in quantity either by rolling or by dies under the hammer;
these parts are brought together in their relative positions in a mould,
heated to a welding heat, and then by a blow of the steam hammer,
furnished with dies, are stamped into a complete and all but finished
wheel.   (1838)

220

Of 419,560 factory operatives of the British Empire in 1839, 192,887,
or nearly half, were under eighteen years of age, and 242,296 of the
female sex, of whom 112,192 were less than eighteen years old.... In
the cotton factories, $50\frac{1}{4}$ per cent, in the woollen mills, $69\frac{1}{2}$ per cent, in
the silk mills, $70\frac{1}{2}$ per cent, in the flax-spinning mills, $70\frac{1}{2}$ per cent of
all the operatives are of the female sex.... Hence follows of necessity
that inversion of the existing social order which, being forced upon
them, has the most ruinous consequences for the workers. The employment of women at once breaks up the family for when the wife spends
twelve or thirteen hours every day in the mill, and the husband works
the same length of time there or elsewhere, what becomes of the
children?   (1839)

221

The population of the manufacturing towns was rapidly thinning, and
the inhabitants who remained were in serious straits. Cobden stated
that in the borough which he represented [Stockport] one house in
every five was empty. Harrowing tales were told of the miserable
poverty to which the factory operatives were reduced. It was affirmed
that men had died at their looms from the exhaustion of famine.

(1841)

[George Stephenson] was thought behind the age because he recommended the rate [of railway trains] to be limited to forty miles an hour. He said, 'I do not like either forty or fifty miles an hour upon any line—I think it an unnecessary speed; and if there is danger upon a railway it is high velocity that creates it. I should say no railway ought to exceed forty miles an hour on the most favourable gradient; but upon a curved line the speed ought not to exceed twenty-four or twenty-five miles an hour.' He had, indeed, constructed for the Great Western Railway an engine capable of running fifty miles an hour with a load, and eighty miles without one. But he never was in favour of a hurricane speed of this sort, believing it could only be accomplished at an unnecessary increase both of danger and expense.   (1841)

223

Messrs Marshall's new mill at Holbeck...had just been erected, and was not yet supplied with machinery. It was built in the style of an Egyptian temple, with an immense chimney like an elongated pyramid. The great roof was supported on iron pillars—there being grass enough on the top for sheep to feed—and the room itself covered five times as much space as Westminster Hall, extending over nearly two acres of ground. It was certainly the largest room in the world, and on this occasion was densely packed. The proceedings, on account of the heterogeneous audience, and the frequent howlings of the Chartists, were very confused.   (1841)

224

The worst situation is that of those workers who have to compete against a machine that is making its way....The manufacturer will not throw out his old apparatus, nor will he sustain the loss upon it; out of the dead mechanism he can make nothing, so he fastens upon the living worker, the universal scapegoat of society. Of all the workers in competition with machinery, the most ill-used are the hand-loom cotton weavers. They receive the most trifling wages, and with full work are not in a position to earn more than 10*s.* a week. One class of woven goods after another is annexed by the power-loom, and hand-weaving is the last refuge of workers thrown out of employment in other branches, so that the trade is always overcrowded.   (1844)   189

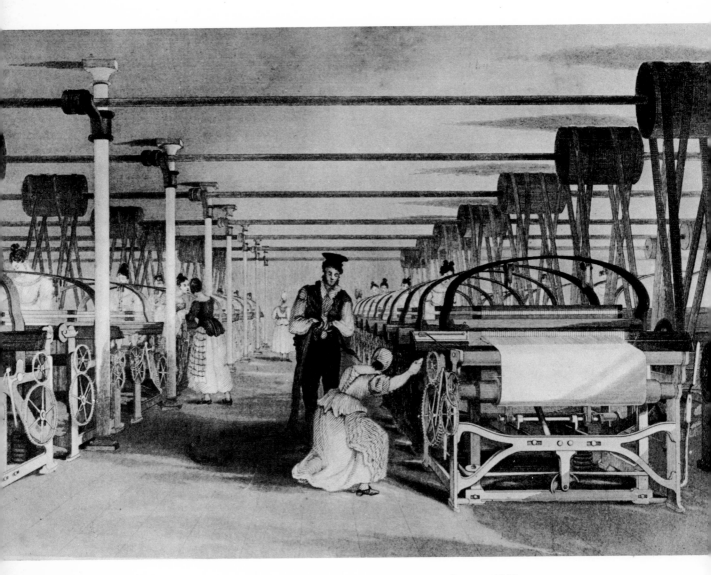

81   *Women engaged in power-loom weaving, c. 1840*

82　*New hydraulic lift at the Victoria Docks, London, 1858*

83   *General view of the new docks at Millwall, London, 1868*

84   *Unloading tea-ships in the East India Docks, London, 1867*

The rapid extension of English industry could not have taken place if England had not possessed in the numerous and impoverished population of Ireland a reserve at command. The Irish had nothing to lose at home, and much to gain in England; and from the time when it became known in Ireland that the East side of St George's Channel offered steady work and good pay for strong arms, every year has brought armies of the Irish hither. It has been calculated [in 1840] that more than a million have already immigrated, and not far from 50,000 still come every year....These people having grown up almost without civilization, accustomed from youth to every sort of privation, rough, intemperate and improvident, bring all their brutal habits with them among a class of the English population which has, in truth, little inducement to cultivate education and morality....These Irishmen who migrate for 4*d.* to England, on the deck of a steamship on which they are often packed like cattle, insinuate themselves everywhere. The worst dwellings are good enough for them; their clothing causes them little trouble, so long as it holds together by a single thread; shoes they know not; their food consists of potatoes and potatoes only; whatever they earn beyond these needs they spend on drink. What does such a race want with high wages? (1844)

226

In no branch of English industry has mechanical ingenuity produced such brilliant results as [in the cotton-printing industry], but in no other has it so crushed the workers. The application of engraved cylinders driven by steam-power, and the discovery of a method of printing four to six colours at once with such cylinders, has as completely superseded hand-work as did the application of machinery to the spinning and weaving of cotton....One man, with the assistance of one child, now does with a machine the work done formerly by 200 block printers; a single machine yields twenty-eight yards of printed cloth per minute. The calico printers are in a very bad way in consequence. (1844)

227

The history of the proletariat in England begins with the second half of the [eighteenth] century, with the invention of the steam-engine and of machinery for working cotton. These inventions gave rise...to an industrial revolution, a revolution which altered the whole civil society; one, the historical importance of which is only now beginning to be recognized. England is the classic soil of this transformation, which was all the mightier, the more silently it proceeded; and England is, therefore, the classic land of its chief product also, the proletariat. Only in England can the proletariat be studied in all its relations and from all sides. (1844)

228

I do not deny that a factory child would produce more in a single day by working twelve hours than by working ten, and by working fifteen hours than by working twelve. But I do deny that a great society in which children work fifteen or even twelve hours a day will, in the life-time of a generation, produce as much as if those children had worked less.... Rely on it, that intense labour, beginning too early in life, continued too long every day, stunting the growth of the mind, leaving no time for healthful exercise, no time for intellectual culture, must impair all those high qualities which have made our country great.
(1846)

229

Railway Bills were granted in heaps. Two hundred and seventy-two additional Acts were passed in 1846. Some authorized the construction of lines running almost parallel to existing railways, in order to afford the public 'the benefits of unrestricted competition'. Locomotive and atmospheric lines, broad gauges and narrow gauge lines, were granted without hesitation. Committees decided without judgment and without discrimination; it was a scramble for Bills, in which the most unscrupulous were the most successful. (1846)

230

Mr Hudson gave a dinner on Thursday to some happy hundreds in the Guildhall of York—but was that all? No, Mr Hudson was yesterday giving, and has for months and years of yesterdays been giving, dinners to hundreds of thousands not less happy than the guests by whom he was surrounded in the Guildhall....He has found the labourers standing to be hired when 'no man hired them', and he has given them employment and good wages and, we repeat it, good dinners—for the labourer who receives from 22*s.* to 23*s.* a week can, according to his habits, command a good dinner....*Two hundred thousand* well-paid labourers, representing, as heads of families, nearly 1 million of men, women and children, all feasting through the bold enterprise of one man, and not feasting for one day or one week, but enjoying abundance from year's end to year's end. Let us hear what man, or class of men, ever before did so much for the population of a country?   (1847)

231

How happily has England been preserved in the midst of these sur-rounding troubles!...Not that her state is altogether prosperous and secure. Wherever you look evils exist within her, threatening future consequences terrible to contemplate. Every year seems to accumulate luxury on the one hand and distress and misery on the other. Who can wonder if even a false hope of bettering their condition should tempt the famishing multitude from their duty? On the whole we do not have to witness much distress about here. Papa's mills give employ-ment to so many, and the people in this village, having both better and more regular pay than the agricultural labourers, get many little comforts about them and are not reduced to starvation on the first disaster. You see books on their tables and muslin blinds in their windows, very often, and altogether a degree of civilization about the place which it is very comforting to witness. I should be miserable if the wealth that built this house had been made by 'grinding the faces of the poor'. As it is we know the very prosperity of this part of the country is bound up in the prosperity of our mills.   (1848)

232

Neither the other officials, nor the shareholders, must hope to escape censure under the cover of a personal onslaught upon Mr Hudson. The system is to blame. It was a system without rule, without order, without even a definite morality. Mr Hudson, having a faculty for amalgamation, and being also successful, found himself in the enjoyment of a great railway despotism, in which...he had...to discover the ethics of railway speculation and management....Mr Hudson's position was not only new to himself, but absolutely a new thing in the world altogether....His system of government and equity was rather intuitive than legal. His colleagues knew this. The shareholders knew it. They would have tolerated it to this day without the smallest objection, but for the unlucky circumstance that Hudson had outlived their success. (1849)

233

'George Hudson,' said Mr Cash, the chairman of the Committee and a member of the Society of Friends, 'wilt thou take a seat? As thou hast the financial department of this Company under thy especial control, thou art required to answer a few questions which the committee will put to thee. Didst thou ever, after the accountants had made up the yearly accounts, alter any of the figures?'

Mr Hudson, in a subdued tone, answered, after a moment's hesitation, 'Well, I may perhaps have added a thousand or two to the next account.'

'Didst thou ever add £10,000?' continued Mr Cash.

'Ten thousand! That is a large sum.'

'It *is* a large sum, and that is the reason why I put the question to thee. Wilt thou give the committee an answer, yea or nay?'

Mr Hudson, in a very subdued tone, and evidently much embarrassed, replied: 'I cannot exactly say what may have been the largest sum I carried to the following account....' (1849)

234

[Hudson's] whole life has been one vast aggregate of avaricious and flagitious jobbing for the accumulation of wealth....The thousands he has duped, and the breaking hearts from whence spring against him curses both loud and deep, shall have ample satisfaction for the injuries they have suffered and the torments they have endured. (1849)

85   *The London–Chatham–Dover Railway experimented with the issuing of cheap workmen's tickets, c. 1865*

86   *New saloon carriage on the London, Brighton and South Coast Railway, 1873*

87   *An express train on the London to Brighton line, 1875*

88   *Handling merchandise at London docks, 1880*

If in a depression you have fifty men out of work they will receive £1015 in a year, and at the same time be used as a whip by your employers to bring your wages down; by sending them to Australia at £20 per head you save £15 and send them to plenty instead of starvation at home; you keep your own wages good by the simple act of clearing the surplus labour out of the market.   (1854)

236

[In] a history of railway management and railway intrigue . . . the doings of projectors and the mysteries of the share market would occupy less space than the analysis of the multiform dishonesties that have been committed since 1845, and the genesis of that elaborate system of tactics by which companies are betrayed into ruinous undertakings that benefit the few at the expense of the many. . . . There are eighty-one directors [of Railway Companies] sitting in Parliament. . . . We have but to look back a few years, and mark the unanimity with which Companies adopted the policy of getting themselves represented in the Legislature, to see that the furtherance of their respective interests—especially in cases of competition—was the incentive.   (1855)

237

July, London. The streets full of perambulators, a baby-carriage quite new to me, whereby the children are propelled by the nurse pushing instead of pulling the little carriage.   (1855)

238

Q. What is a steam-carriage?
A. A carriage provided with a steam-engine, which is made to turn the wheels.
Q. What is a steam-boat?
A. A ship provided with a steam-engine, the force of which turns wheels that act on the water like the oars of a boat. . . .

Q. What is a McAdamized road?

A. A road formed of small stones of uniform size and weight, so as to bind together in a smooth road.

Q. How fast is conveyance by each of these means?

A. By a steam-vessel, twelve or fifteen miles an hour; by a steam-carriage on a rail-road, thirty to sixty miles...and by a stage-coach on McAdamized roads, eight or nine miles.   (1856)

239

One way in which self-culture may be degraded is by regarding it too exclusively as a means of 'getting on'. Viewed in this light, it is unquestionable that education is one of the best investments of time and labour....

Self culture may not, however, end in eminence....The great majority of men, in all times, however enlightened, must necessarily be engaged in the ordinary avocations of industry; and no degree of culture which can be conferred upon the community at large will ever enable them—even were it desirable, which it is not—to get rid of the daily work of society, which must be done. But this, we think, may also be accomplished. We can elevate the condition of labour by allying it to noble thoughts, which confer a grace upon the lowliest as well as the highest rank.   (1859)

240

As soon as one mill is at work, occupying two hundred hands, we try, by means of it, to set another mill at work, occupying four hundred. That is all simple and comprehensible enough—but what is it to come to? How many mills do we want? Or do we indeed want no end of mills?...Last week I drove twenty miles from Rochdale to Bolton Abbey....Naturally, the valley has been one of the most beautiful in the Lancashire hills; one of the far-away solitudes full of old shepherds' ways of life. At this time there are not—I speak deliberately and I believe quite literally—there are not, I think, more than a thousand yards of road to be traversed anywhere, without passing a furnace or mill.   (1859)

A meeting of the principal West End tradesmen has just been held, for the purpose of taking into consideration the proposition for closing their establishments on Saturdays at such an hour as will afford a half-holiday on the afternoon of that day to the young persons whom they employ. The definite proposal is that the shops throughout London generally should close on Saturday afternoon not later than 5 o'clock between Lady Day and Michaelmas, and not later than 4 o'clock between Michaelmas and Lady Day. There is a distinct advantage in this arrangement, which may easily be recognized, in opposition to that proposed by what is called the Early Closing Movement. It matters comparatively little to the young men engaged by the various silk-mercers, etc., whether or not the shops are closed one hour sooner or later on five days of the week, so that they have their Sundays to themselves and a clear half-holiday on the Saturday. Of course, they would be glad to have the extra hour of freedom, although we doubt if a number of young men let loose upon the streets of London at an early hour would employ that additional period of leisure in a way very advantageous to themselves. They would not be liberated so that they could take a walk into the country or pull upon the river, or go to drill with the rifle corps, or engage in any other manly exercise, and we believe that they would be better pleased to do a full day's work for five days in the week if they could have on the sixth a real half-holiday. Young men will then naturally seek to throw off the weariness of the week's confinement by exercise of a creditable and rational kind.

(1860)

242

28 March 1872. As I came away from the school this afternoon a man standing by the finger-post accosted me and asked if I had any work for him to do. He said he was a Shropshire man named Wilding from the town of Bridgenorth. He was by trade a hatter and was cleaning hats and coats along the road to help him down to Cardiff where there was a manufactory where he hoped to get work. He was penniless he said. He had not been able to get a piece of work to do all day though he had tried hard. He was fasting and wet through. 'Feel my coat, Sir', he said. I felt his coat. It was drenched, soaked with the pitiless rain.

(1872)

12 May. While reading in the herald to Day on the subject on shorter houers of Labour I was Reminded of A cercomstance that came under my hone notis when the 10 hours sistom Began in the cotton mills in Lancashire.... I was Minding a masheen with 30 treds in it I was then maid to mind 2 of 30 treds each with one shilling Advance of wages wich was 5s. for one and 6s. for tow with an increes of speed and with improved mecheens in A few years I was minding tow mecheens with tow 100 treds each and Dubel speed for 9s. perweek so that in our improved condation we had to turn out some 100 weght per day and we went as if the Devel was After us for 10 houers per day and with that comparetive small Advance in money and the feemals have often Been carred out fainting what with the heat and hard work and those that could not keep up must go and make room for a nother and all this is Done in Christian England and then we are tould to Be content in the station of Life to wich the Lord as places us But I say the Lord never Did place us there so we have no Right to Be content.... (1873)

244

As we drove down the hill a little further towards Bewdley...my host asked me if I would like to see 'nailing'.... He took me into a little cottage where were two women at work, one about seventeen or eighteen, the other perhaps four or five and thirty; this last intelligent of feature as well could be; and both, gentle and kind,—each with hammer in right hand, pincers in left (heavier hammer poised over her anvil, and let fall at need by the touch of her foot on a treadle like that of a common grindstone). Between them a small forge, fed to constant brightness by the draught through the cottage, above whose roof its chimney rose: in front of it, on a little ledge, the glowing lengths of cut iron rod, to be dealt with at speed.... Four strokes with the hammer in the hand: one ponderous and momentary blow ordered of the balanced mass by the touch of the foot; and the forged nail fell aside, finished, on its proper heap;—level-headed, wedge pointed, a thousand lives soon to depend daily on its driven grip of the iron way....

The wages of the matron, I found, were 8*s.* a week;—her husband, otherwise and variously employed, could make 16. Three shillings a week for rent and taxes left, as I count...£55 a year, on which they had to feed and clothe themselves and their six children; eight souls in their little Worcestershire ark. (1877)

89 *The industrial aspect of Leeds from Richmond Hill, 1885*

245

A highly gifted and carefully educated man shall...squint at a sheet of paper, and the results of that squint shall set a vast number of well-fed, contented operatives...turning crank-handles for ten hours a day, bidding them keep what gifts and education they may have been born with for their—I was going to say leisure hours, but...if I were to work ten hours a day at work I despised and hated I should spend my leisure, I hope, in political agitation, but I fear—in drinking....Well, from this system are to come threefold blessings—food and clothing, poorish lodgings and a little leisure for the operatives, enormous riches to the capitalists that rent them, together with moderate riches to the squinter on the paper; and lastly, very decidedly lastly, abundance of cheap art for the operatives and crank-turners to buy.   (*c.* 1879)

246

Sir,—I believe the inhabitants of London are under the impression that letters posted for delivery within the metropolitan district commonly reach their destination within, at the outside, three hours of the time of postage. I myself, however, have constantly suffered from irregularities in the delivery of letters, and I have now got two instances of neglect which I should really like to have cleared up.

I posted a letter in the Gray's Inn post office on Saturday, at half-past 1 o'clock, addressed to a person living close to Westminster Abbey, which was not delivered till next 9 o'clock the same evening; and I posted another letter in the same post office, addressed to the same place, on Monday morning (6 May) before 9 o'clock, which was not delivered till past 4 o'clock in the afternoon. Now, sir, why is this? If there is any good reason why letters should not be delivered in less than eight hours after their postage, let the state of the case be understood: but the belief that one can communicate with another person in two or three hours whereas in reality the time required is eight or nine, may be productive of the most disastrous consequences.

I am, Sir, your obedient servant,

7 May   K.

(1881)

247

The Co-operative System

The object of this system may be described as the furnishing of members of a trading association, formed for the purpose, with genuine and moderately priced goods on the principle of ready-money payments, the cheapness being secured by economy of management and by contentment with small profits. Notwithstanding the opposition of retail and even of wholesale dealers it has of late years made astonishingly rapid progress in London, where there are now about thirty 'Co-operative stores' carrying on an immense trade.   (1900)

BELIEF

90 *'The Scapegoat', by W. Holman Hunt*

Belief—wholehearted, unquestioning belief—in things incapable of proof, was a notable capacity of the Victorians. Its natural and proper sphere was religion, but the same attitude of mind spread into every field. An agnostic was no gentle disbeliever in the unproved, but as violent a bigot as any Tractarian or Plymouth Brother. The dignitaries of the Church preached their doctrines with no little arrogance. Carlyle, Ruskin, Gladstone and many other laymen spoke on any subject with an authority usually reserved for great churchmen in an Age of Faith; and they were reverently listened to by men and women of good intelligence, if but little formal training in logic.

Such free-thinkers as there were gained their inspiration from France and Germany, and their followers from the half-educated, and were not really part of the English scene. Only in certain scientific circles, mostly with a Cambridge or Quaker background, did a slow and almost Belief tacit demand for scientific evidence begin to make itself felt. (One of the most remarkable facts about Lyell's *Principles of Geology*, of which the publication began in 1830, is that he politely and consistently ignores the theological point of view.) Even at the end of the nineteenth century this demand was hardly recognized, and was certainly not general. In Oxford fifty years ago 'pragmatism' was still a pejorative word. There was no organized scientific outlook demanding proof of everything by mathematics or experiment to challenge the dominance of a religious outlook that was content to rest a philosophy upon faith. It is impossible to understand Victorian thought except in terms of a received Christianity.

The reign of Victoria witnessed very considerable changes in the position of the Established Church and the Christian universities. Just before she ascended the throne, a system of commutation of tithes had been effected and the Ecclesiastical Commissioners had been incorporated to deal with the estates and endowments of the Church. In 1854 the University Reform Bill made orthodox Anglicanism no longer a necessary qualification for matriculation and the Bachelor's degree at Oxford and Cambridge. But since the M.A. was given, in mediaeval fashion, in the name of the Trinity and Holy Mother Church, orthodoxy was still required for the further degree that carried a vote in Convocation. In 1869 the Anglican Church in Ireland was disestablished, but it retained all endowments received since 1660.

In 1870 (the year in which Keble College was founded), the revision of the Bible was officially undertaken, with a Unitarian among the revisers.

In the Church of England the broad division between Evangelical and High Church was valid for the whole of the Victorian Age. Newman, in his *Prophetical Office of the Church*, published in the year before Victoria's accession, had laid down the theory which the Oxford Movement was to animate. On the other hand, the ministry of Charles Simeon at Holy Trinity, Cambridge, up to his death in 1836, had given new life to the Evangelical tradition that England had inherited from the Puritans. In 1846 the British and Foreign Bible Society received donations of £101,305 and issued 1,441,651 Bibles.

The Bible, indeed, was far more important to the Victorians than we always remember. A learned high churchman might read the Fathers as a learned Evangelical might read the Institutes of Calvin and Fox, but they were as one in basing all their arguments on the

Belief Word of Scripture, considered without regard to the circumstances in which it had been written and with little consciousness of the possibility of change through many translations. It was easy for parsons who were not trained thinkers (and were, indeed, imperfectly trained theologians) to bandy texts. Yet this common basis did not secure unity.

It is pathetic to see truly good men such as Keble and Pusey spending their time and energies on the tittles of ecclesiastical legislation and theological interpretation, when innumerable Christians in Britain were suffering hunger, ignorance and deprivation. F. D. Maurice, who had a strong sense of the Christian duty of education, was in 1853 ejected from the Chair of Theology at King's College because he had questioned the doctrine of Eternal Punishment.

Both High Church and Evangelical could be completely humourless: About 1848 Pusey seriously considered giving up smiling—except perhaps to a child—as a reasonable Christian mortification. On the Evangelical side, I know of a man, a member of a distinguished legal family, who used to read exactly two inches of the Bible at family prayers, regardless of the sense. It is in some ways significant that Dean Stanley was totally tone-deaf, and that he, and Canon Barnett, and Canon Barnett's wife, were all colour-blind. It is painfully interesting to compare the attitude of two enthusiastic Christians—Dr Pusey and General Booth of the Salvation Army—at much the same time. Pusey argues on the grounds of the opinion of St Basil that a man must never marry his deceased wife's sister; and Booth spends his time on thinking out how the output of empty tins from urban households can be employed to the good of the poor.

It is impossible for anyone who reads any of the religious controversy of the time not to have a sense of quibbling, of pettiness and of insignificance in the theologians, in comparison with the honest and creative thought of the scientists and of the—relatively few—authentic historians. Their devotion to truth involved an intellectual modesty which seems absent from the work of the theologians. Yet even clerical headmasters had their scruples. Arnold of Rugby hated it when any pupil of his proposed to read for the Bar, for he considered that advocacy was incompatible with the pursuit of truth.

The Church was traditionally the vocation of the third son of a good family. There was an immense range of stipend: good livings (usually kept in the family of the patron) could be worth £2000 a year or more; curates could be thankful for £60 or £80, and do all the work of the nominal incumbent. There were many Victorian parsons who were pious, learned, modest and devoted; but they did not often receive honourable and profitable preferment.

Only a few great Anglicans can take their place as Victorian saints. Keble, undoubtedly the greatest of them, had simplicity, wisdom and holiness, balanced by the more sophisticated virtues of scholarship and poetic skill, and the secular qualities of loving-kindness and common sense.

The shade of religious opinion in a family might affect its whole culture: high church people like the Hares would travel habitually in Europe, whereas Evangelical and nonconformist families of comfortable income would consider that to go to a Catholic country—and especially to Rome—was to venture on a trial by fire that they were proudly unwilling to undergo. Similarly a man's beliefs conditioned his influence; the public importance of men of second-rate intellect, such as Kingsley and Maurice, depended in great measure on their earnestness; while the religiosity of the times prevented such a great man as Matthew Arnold from being fully appreciated. Pusey—a dull man usually prepared to delegate in matters of scholarship—and Darwin, a man of the most direct and lively mind, original in everything, were almost equally famous and influential in the decade of the sixties. In the war of 1870 English sympathy was mainly with Prussia, because, although the country was indubitably the aggressor, it was not Roman Catholic.

The exclusion of women not only from the ministry but also from the councils of the Church of England meant that a number of the most able churchwomen—who sometimes knew as much theology and as much Greek as their pastors—were perpetually dissatisfied, even if they did not admit or know the cause of their dissatisfaction. It helped to encourage a number of movements within the Church not under Church discipline, but run by converted Jews or Copts or Assyrian Christians, who were more grateful for the attention of these ladies—and more skilful in expressing their gratitude for their alms—than the incumbents of their parishes.

Outside the Church of England there was much activity. In 1850 (the year in which Manning joined the Church of Rome), for the first time the Pope appointed bishops to English Catholic sees; and in 1895 the splendid Roman Catholic cathedral at Westminster was begun. A tendency to revivalism in the dissenting churches culminated in Moody and Sankey's 'Great Mission' of 1873.

In many ways the sixties were a turning point in Victorian history. 1860 saw the publication of *Essays and Reviews*, that brought some

Belief fresh air into theology, and 1865 witnessed the foundation of the Salvation Army, that made human happiness, if only among the dregs of society, a factor in the ethics of religion.

Science in the Victorian age was in the hands of amateurs, for there was remarkably little professional training available. Amateurs are characterized by an unworldly devotion to their subject, by an empiric approach to it, by a learning that is not academic, and, often enough, by a certain failure in the sense of proportion, that is a consequence of their enthusiasm and their isolation. Some of the discoverers of physical laws and processes were men such as Faraday, who were self-educated empiricists. The great biologists, such as Darwin and Galton, were observers—naturalists—rather than experimenters. The geologists and archaeologists were amateurs: Pitt-Rivers and Murchison were soldiers, Prestwich a wine merchant, Hugh Miller a stone-mason, John Evans a paper manufacturer, John Lubbock a banker, Roach Smith a pharmacist. Wollaston Franks's only formal training was as a mathematician. Lyell, it is true, studied geology at Oxford, and Kelvin mathematics at Cambridge. Huxley and Lister were trained medical men; but Florence Nightingale was the completest amateur of them all. It was the amateur travellers and anthropologists such as Darwin and Haddon who provided the material for such a synthesis as Frazer's *Golden Bough* (first published in 1891), that owed nothing to the Christian cosmogony.

Perhaps in consequence of this amateurishness and of the paucity of research institutions, England failed to produce a Pasteur or a Virchow; neither did she produce a philosopher of European stature, but she made evolution a scientific fact and completely changed surgery, nursing and public health. Simpson used chloroform as an anaesthetic in 1847; Lister a germicidal spray on operation wounds in 1865; and John Snow helped to end the cholera epidemic of 1861—the last of three pandemics—by getting the vestry of St James's to remove the handle of the parish pump. He had never seen the cholera bacillus, but he had arrived at the conclusion that the disease was spread by tainted water.

Public Health was indeed in need of progress. In 1848 the cholera reached London and Edinburgh in October; by the end of the year 1105 were dead in England alone. In the next year, in the week ending 8 September, 2026 people died in London of the disease. In 1848, in spite of vaccination, 6903 people died of smallpox in Britain. The Public Health Act of 1848, which dealt with sewers and drains, was the first sanitary measure in English law; but it must be remembered that it could only be applied by the General Board of Health to any locality if either the Local Authority, or ten per cent of the rate-payers, demanded it, or if the death rate was above 23 per thousand. The great metropolitan and provincial hospitals did much, but were not always easy of access; I know how one artisan family sent their blind child to be examined at Moorfields about 1870 by selling the ancestral silver spoons.

Parson Kilvert, living in the sixties and seventies in a country parish on the borders of Wales and Herefordshire, is for ever writing of parishioners ill with consumption, madness, bronchitis, fever and broken limbs, and hardly ever suggests that they are under a doctor's care; and I can myself remember things not much better in North Buckinghamshire at the turn of this century.

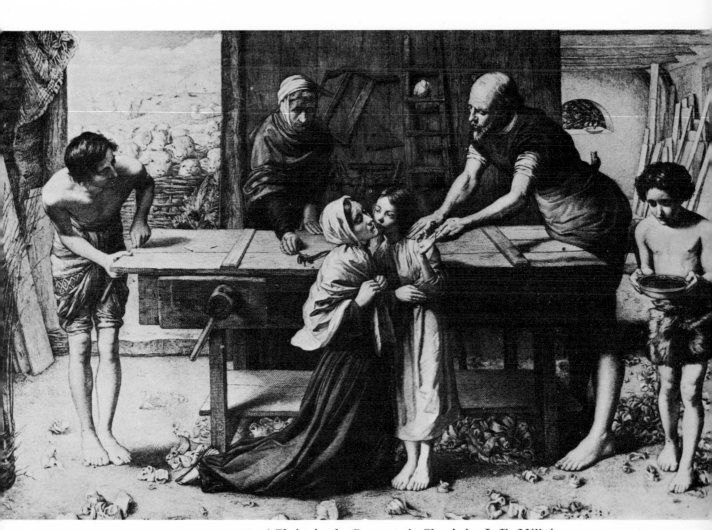

91 *'Christ in the Carpenter's Shop', by J. E. Millais*

92 *The Oxford Museum, from a photograph of 1858*

93   *The Anglican Cathedral, Truro, Cornwall*

94   *Professor T. H. Huxley, from a photograph, c. 1890*

95   *Cardinal Newman, from a photograph by H. Barraud, 1887*

96   *Charles Darwin, by Marian Collier, 1878*

I want to petition against the Jew Bill. . . .I want to take my stand on my favourite principle, that the world is made up of Christians and non-Christians, with all the former we should be one, with none of the latter. . . .The Jews are strangers in England and have no more claim to legislate for it than a lodger has to share with the landlord in the management of his house. (1836)

249

We have nothing here [at Chelsea Rectory] but clergymen [very good and sensible men but] talking of nothing but parochial schools, and duties, and vestries, and curates, etc., etc., etc. . . .The girls here have got their heads crammed full of schools, and district visiting, and baby-linen, and penny clubs. Confound!!! and going about among the most abominable scenes of filth, wretchedness, and indecency, to visit the poor and read the Bible to them. My own mother says the places they go to are fit for no girl to see, and that they should not know such things exist. (1837)

250

Dr Andrews' was the Londonian chapel in its perfect type, definable as accurately as a Roman basilica—an oblong, flat-ceiled barn lighted by windows with semi-circular heads, brick arched, filled by small-paned glass held by iron bars, like fine threaded halves of cobwebs; galleries propped on iron pipes, up both sides; pews, well shut in, each of them, by partitions of plain deal, and neatly latched deal doors, filling the barn floor, all but its two lateral straw-matted passages; pulpit sublimely isolated, central from sides and clear of altar rails at end; a stout, four-legged box of well-grained wainscot, high as the level of the front galleries, and decorated with a cushion of crimson velvet, padded 6 inches thick, with gold tassels at the corners; which was a great resource to me when I was tired of the sermon, because I liked watching the rich colour of the folds and creases that came in it when the clergyman thumped it. (*c.* 1837) 219

Whether you go to India or to any other foreign country, the first and great point, I think, is to turn your thoughts to the edification of the Church already in existence—that is, the English or Christian societies as distinct from the Hindoos. Unless the English and the half-caste people can be brought into a good state, how can you get on with the Hindoos? Again, I am inclined to think that greater good might be done by joining a young English settlement, than by missionary work among the heathen. (1840)

252

Littlemore. March 17th, 1840. Since I have been here an idea has revived in my mind...of building a monastic house in the place, and coming to live in it myself....It has long been a distress that I know so little of my parishioners in Oxford, but tradespeople it is next to impossible to know, considering how they have been educated—at least impossible to me. It has pained me much to be preaching and doing little more than preaching....

I am quite of opinion, first, that such a scheme cannot begin in Oxford, nor in London or other great towns. Next I think we must begin with a complete type or specimen which may *preach* to others. I am sanguine that if we could once get one set up at Littlemore it would set the example both in great towns, and for female societies. (1840)

253

In the course of my inquiries on the subject of muscular Christians, their works and wages, a fact has forced itself on my attention. Side by side with these muscular Christians, and apparently claiming some sort of connexion with them, have risen up another set of persons. I call [them] 'musclemen' as distinct from muscular Christians; the only point in common between the two being that both hold it to be a good thing to have strong and well-exercised bodies, ready to be put at the shortest notice to any work of which bodies are capable, and to do it well. Here all likeness ends; for the 'muscleman' seems to have no belief whatever as to the purposes for which his body has been given him, except some hazy idea that it is to go up and down the world with

220 him belabouring men and captivating women for his benefit or pleasure,

at once the servant and fomenter of those fierce and brutal passions
which he seems to think it a necessity, and rather a fine thing than
otherwise, to obey. Whereas, so far as I know, the least of the muscular
Christians has hold of the old chivalrous and Christian belief, that a
man's body is given him to be trained and brought into subjection,
and then used for the protection of the weak, the advancement of all
righteous causes and the subduing of the earth which God has given to
the children of men. He does not hold that mere strength or activity
are in themselves worthy of any respect or worship...[though] he
would probably himself, as a matter of taste, prefer the man who can
lift a hundredweight round his head with his little finger to the man
who can construct a string of perfect *sorites* or expound the doctrine of
'contradictory inconceivables'.   (*c.* 1840)

254

I don't know why Hendon should have asked me. He can't think me
a likely card for a convert, I should think. At any rate, he asked me to
wine, and I went as usual. Everything was in capital style (it don't
seem to be any part of their creed, mind you, to drink bad wine), and
awfully gentlemanly and decorous....There was a piano in one corner
and muslin curtains. I give you my word, muslin curtains, besides the
stiff ones....I counted three sorts of scents on the mantel-piece, besides Eau de Cologne. But I could have stood it all well enough if it
hadn't been for their talk. From one thing to another they got to
cathedrals, and one of them called St Paul's 'a disgrace to a Christian
city'. I couldn't stand that, you know. I was always bred to respect
St Paul's; weren't you?...I plumped out that St Paul's was the
finest cathedral in England. You'd have thought I had said lying was
one of the cardinal virtues. One or two just treated me to a sort of
pitying sneer, but my neighbours were down upon me with a vengeance.
I stuck to my text though, and they drove me into saying that I liked
the Ratcliffe [*sic*] more than any building in Oxford, which I don't
believe I do, now I come to think of it. So when they couldn't get me
to budge for their talk, they took to telling me that everybody who
knew anything about church architecture was against me....[I] said
I didn't care a straw for them...there was no right or wrong in the
matter, and I had as good a right to my opinion as Pugin—or whatever
his name is—and the rest.   (*c.* 1840)   221

The [College] chapel is a quaint little place. It just holds us all comfortably. The attendance is regular enough but I don't think the men care about it a bit in general. Several I can see bring in Euclids and other lecture books, and the service is gone through at a great pace. I couldn't think at first why some of the men seemed so uncomfortable and stiff about the legs at the morning service, but I find that they are the hunting set, and come in with pea-coats over their pinks, and trousers over their leather breeches and top-boots, which accounts for it. There are a few others who seem very devout and bow a good deal, and turn towards the altar at different parts of the service. These are of the Oxford High Church School, I believe, but I shall soon find out more about them. On the whole, I feel less at home at present, I am sorry to say, in the chapel, than anywhere else.   (*c.* 1840)

256

Eternal Light! eternal Light!
  How pure the soul must be,
When, placed within Thy searching sight,
It shrinks not, but with calm delight
  Can live and look on Thee.

The spirits that surround Thy throne
  May bear the burning bliss;
But that is surely theirs alone,
Since they have never, never known
  A fallen world like this.

O how shall I, whose native sphere
  Is dark, whose mind is dim,
Before the ineffable appear,
And on my naked spirit bear
  The uncreated beam?

There is a way for man to rise
  To that sublime abode:
An offering and a sacrifice,
A Holy Spirit's energies,
  An advocate with God.

These, these prepare us for the sight
  Of holiness above:
The sons of ignorance and night
May dwell in the eternal light
  Through the eternal love!

                              (*c.* 1840)

257

If, during a period so vast as to be scarce expressible by figures, the creatures now human have been rising, by *almost* infinitesimals from compound microscopic cells...until they have at length become the men and women whom we see around us, we must hold either the monstrous belief, that all the vitalities, whether those of monads or of mites, of fishes or of reptiles, of birds or of beasts, are individually immortal and undying, or that human souls are *not* so....And thus, though the development theory be not atheistic, it is at least practically tantamount to atheism. For, if man be a dying creature, restricted in his existence to the present scene of things, what does it really matter to him, for any one moral purpose, whether there be a God or no? (1841)

258

[Chapels] are erected by men who ponder between a mortgage, a railroad or a chapel, as the best investment of their money, and who, when they have resolved on relying on the persuasive eloquence of a cushion-thumping, popular preacher, erect four walls with apertures for windows, cram the same full of seats, which they readily let; and so greedy after self are these chapel-raisers, that they form dry and spacious vaults underneath which are soon occupied at a good rent by some wine and brandy merchant. (1841)

259

The crowds which make their way through the suburbs of our great cities toward the country on the Lord's day, especially in the neighbourhood of London, convey a most unfavourable impression with regard to the condition of the religious feeling in the case of a large proportion of our people, both in the lower and in the middle classes.

                              (1843)

Newman's conversion...which swept the leader of the Tractarians, with most of his followers, out of [Oxford], was an epoch in the history of the university. It was a deliverance from the nightmare which had oppressed Oxford for fifteen years....Probably there was no period in our history during which, I do not say science and learning, but the ordinary study of the classics, was so profitless or at so low an ebb as during the period of the Tractarian controversy. By the secessions of 1845 this was extinguished in a moment, and from that moment dates the regeneration of the university....We were startled when we came to reflect that the vast domain of physical science had been hitherto wholly excluded from our programme. (1845)

261

In the present rage for Gothic churches there is too much of ecclesiolatry—of a maudlin sort of devotion towards the buildings themselves as edifices mystically sanctified, which require to be mystically planned, in as strict accordance as may be with the religious fancies of our forefathers....Our modern Gothic architects...have got into a wrong, perverse and unnatural course, inasmuch as they strive to substitute reproduction for production and pique themselves on fidelity, or what they take to be fidelity, or imitation; which unlucky ambition may render them clever mimics, but never great performers. (1845)

262

Sermon at Fast-Day for Irish Famine

Whatever amendments there may have been among us, luxury and self-indulgence have been increasing among us; no class has been contented with the expenditure of their forefathers; new luxuries have invaded us; luxuries have become comforts, and comforts have become necessaries and our idols. In its turn, luxury is the parent of covetousness; and covetousness of unjust gain, and of the grinding of the poor. We *will* not limit our self-indulgence; and so in order to obtain it cheaply, we pare down the wages of our artisans. (1846)

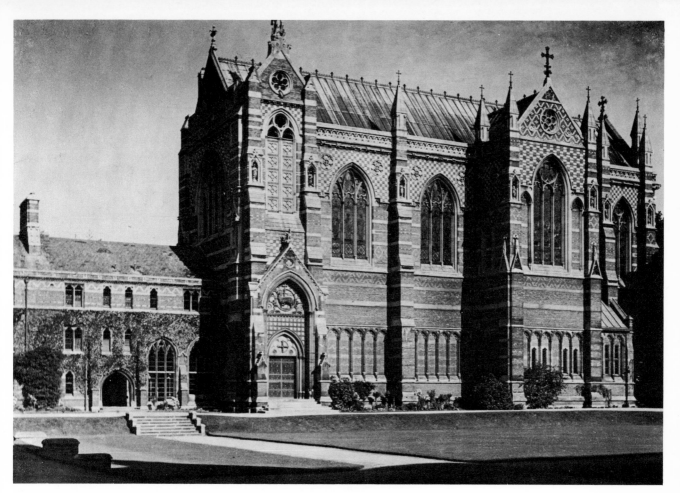

97   *Keble College, Oxford*

98   *Wesleyan Chapel, Blackpool, Lancashire*

99   *Sunday observance, c. 1900*

100   *The Altar, Brompton Oratory, London*

Considering how little sympathy I have with the clergy, for I never hear a sermon scarcely which does not seem equally divided between truth and falsehood, it seems like a kind of treachery to be one of them. But I really believe that treachery to the clergy is loyalty to the Church, and that if religion is to be saved at all it must be through the laity and statesmen, etc., not through the clergy.   (1846)

264

A Society for the Distribution of Religious Prints
amongst the Middle Classes, the Poor,
and Charity Schools.
With Lord John Russell as a Patron.   (1848)

265

I was so ill when we returned home...that it is astonishing my health should not have been considered a primary object. A few weeks of healthy life on moors or by the seaside...would probably have restored me; a visit to German baths might have cured me, and saved years of ill-health. Had the family only had any practical common-sense! But, on religious grounds, it was thought wrong to contend against 'the wonderful leadings of God's Providence'—pain was 'sent' to be endured, sickness as a tractor to draw its victims to heaven; and all simple and rational means of restoration to a healthy and healthful life were disregarded.   (1849)

266

With the exception of one earnest minded Evangelical and a young Anglo-Catholic priest, I cannot say much for the numerous neighbouring clergy. Indifferentism is the prevailing feeling among them, and the farm, the Petty Sessions, and the Union Board are their occupations. They live like educated and well-disposed country gentlemen and seem to have no taste for the 'work of the ministry'.   (1851)

In proportion as there is hope that science should be religious, I should be glad to see science established at Oxford....The problem of Oxford is not to furnish a mere stimulant for intellectual study, but so to impart knowledge and to discipline the mind, as to form (by God's grace) Christian men.   (1851)

268

God did not teach [man] words, as one of us teaches a parrot, from without; but gave him a capacity, and then evoked the capacity which He gave. Here, as in everything else that concerns the primitive constitution, the great original institutes of humanity, our best and truest lights are to be gotten from the study of the three first chapters of Genesis; and you will observe that there it is not God who imposed the first names on the creatures, but Adam—Adam, however, at the direct suggestion of the Creator.   (1851)

269

Robbed, oppressed, and thrust aside, Catholics in these islands have not been in a condition for centuries to attempt the sort of education which is necessary for the man of the world, the statesman, the land-holder or the opulent gentleman. Their legitimate stations, duties, employments, have been taken from them.   (1852)

270

It bothers me when the clergymen say that everybody ought to think alike and follow the one true way, forgetting that it is they who want people to think alike, that is, as they do....I am sure that when Christ talked about 'My words' He means His own, not the Bible, as grannie says.   (1852)

271

The Genealogies of Our Lord and Saviour Jesus Christ, as contained in the Gospels of St Matthew and St Luke, reconciled with each other and with the Genealogy of the House of David, from Adam to the close of the Canon of the Old Testament and shown to be in harmony with the true Chronology of the Times. By Lord Arthur Hervey, M.A., Rector of Ickworth with Horringer. 8vo. cloth, 10*s.* 6*d.*   (1855)

Think of their finding flint axes and arrowheads at Abbeville in conjunction with bones of Elephants and Rhinoceroses 40 feet below the surface in a bed of drift. In this bone cave in Devonshire now being excavated by the Geological Society they say they have found flint arrowheads among the bones, and the same is reported of a cave in Sicily. I can hardly believe it. It will make my Ancient Britons quite modern if man is carried back in England to the days when Elephants, Rhinoceroses, Hippopotamuses and Tigers were also inhabitants of the country.   (1859)

273

The longer I live, the more obvious it is to me that the most sacred act of a man's life is to say and to feel: 'I believe such and such to be true.' All the greatest rewards and all the heaviest penalties of existence cling about that act. The universe is one and the same throughout; and if the condition of my success in unravelling some little difficulty of anatomy or physiology is that I shall rigorously refuse to put faith in that which does not rest on sufficient evidence, I cannot believe that the great mysteries of existence will be laid open to me on other terms. It is no use to me to talk to me of analogies and probabilities. I know what I mean when I say I believe in the law of the inverse squares, and I will not rest my life and my hopes upon weaker convictions. I dare not if I would.   (1860)

274

Shall we begin by taking it as a general principle—that all disease, at some period or other of its course, is more or less a reparative process, not necessarily accompanied with suffering: an effort of nature to remedy a process of poisoning or of decay, which has taken place weeks, months, sometimes years beforehand, unnoticed, the termination of the disease being then...determined?...The art of nursing, as now practised, seems to be expressly constituted to unmake what God had made disease to be, viz. a reparative process.   (1860)

It is...an awkward prospect which we have before us, if we are to look forward now to a struggle of a class of philosophical clergy with the creed of their congregations. There are many minute distinctions of doctrine about which these congregations do not care, but there is one authority upon which they do stand, and that is the authority of Scripture. The Bible, with its facts and its doctrines, naturally interpreted, is undeniably the religion of Protestant England. Our clergy, then, have a considerable latitude allowed them, but any theory which brings them into collision with the Bible, and which forces them to adopt a peculiar mode of interpreting the Bible, depriving it of its character as a record of certain actual facts connected with the foundation of our faith, idealizing these facts, and, in short, making the Bible a totally different thing from what the common belief supposes it to be—such a theory does appear to unfit a clergyman for the practical duties of a parish priest; because he is, in fact, in diametrical opposition to his parishioners with respect to the very basis of Christianity and the very foundation of their faith. He is in a false relation to them, which, whether clearly known by them or not, is a fundamental defect in his position: and if he preaches openly what he thinks there is no parish in England in which he could stay a week. (1861)

276

Science seems to me to teach in the highest and strongest manner the great truth which is embodied in the Christian conception of entire surrender to the will of God. Sit down before facts as a little child, be prepared to give up every preconceived notion, follow humbly wherever and to whatever abysses nature leads, or you shall learn nothing. I have only begun to learn content and peace of mind since I resolved at all risks to do this. (1863)

277

Even leaving Mr Darwin's views aside the whole analogy of natural operations furnishes so complete and crushing an argument against the intervention of any but what are termed secondary causes, in the production of all the phenomena of the universe; that, in view of the

Belief intimate relations between Man and the rest of the living world, and between the forces of the latter and all other forces, I can see no excuse for doubting that all are co-ordinated terms of Nature's great progression, from the formless to the formed—from the inorganic to the organic—from blind force to conscious intellect and will.   (1863)

278

Whatever system of organs be studied, the comparison of their modifications in the ape series leads to one and the same result—that the structural differences which separate Man from the Gorilla and the Chimpanzee are not so great as those which separate the Gorilla from the lower apes.   (1863)

279

I have had, and continue to have, the most exquisite delight in the Bible beyond any past experience I ever felt. All that dead time when I read without interest, merely because I ought to do so, is now repaid me, and God brings the passages back to memory with the power of the Spirit.   (1867)

280

The people who have sons or husbands in the [Franco-Prussian] war have their attention drawn to God, now that sorrow has come on them. They know that He directs the bullet and that He alone rules; all men believe this in their hearts, so they call on Him. In their need they search themselves and subdue their evil natures as He gives them strength....The war, when looked on with respect to individual families, is not worse than everyday life....All these things are beautiful and glorious in the extreme. They come from the *Rest of God* into which we enter when we cease to think for ourselves.   (1870)

101   *The British Museum, Natural History, South Kensington, London, 1873–80*

102 *The British Museum, London*

281

It...appears to be very important to success in science, that a man should have an able mother. I believe the reason to be, that a child so circumstanced has the good fortune to be delivered from the narrowing partisan influences of home education....We are inclined to look upon an honest, unshrinking pursuit of truth as something irreverent. We are indignant when others pry into our idols.... Women are far more strongly influenced by these feelings than are men: they are blinder partisans and more servile followers of custom. Happy are they whose mothers did not intensify their naturally slavish dispositions in childhood, by the frequent use of phrases such as 'Do not ask questions about this or that for it is wrong to doubt'; but who showed them, by practice and teaching, that inquiry may be absolutely free without being irreverent, that reverence for truth is the parent of free inquiry, and that indifference or insincerity in the pursuit of truth

234 is the most degrading of sins.   (1870)

The sole object of this work is to consider, first, whether man, like every other species, is descended from some pre-existing form; secondly, the manner of his development; and thirdly, the value of the differences between the so-called races of man....The high antiquity of man has recently been demonstrated by the labours of a host of eminent men, beginning with Boucher de Perthes, and this is the indispensable basis for understanding his origin....Professor Huxley, in the opinion of most competent judges, has conclusively shown that in even visible character man differs less from the higher apes, than these do from the lower members of the same order of Primates.

(1871)

283

Accurate and minute measurement seems to the non-scientific imagination a less lofty and dignified work than looking for something new. But nearly all the grandest discoveries of science have been but the rewards of accurate measurement and patient, long continued labour on the minute sifting of numerical results.   (1871)

284

One day when I was working from the beautiful maid of honour in Veronese's picture, I was struck by the gorgeousness of life which the world seems to be constituted to develop, when it is made the best of. The band was playing some passages of brilliant music at the time, and this music blended so thoroughly with Veronese's splendour, the beautiful notes seeming to form one whole with the lovely forms and colours and powerful human creatures. Can it be possible that all this power and beauty is adverse to the honour of the maker of it? Has God made faces beautiful and limbs strong, and created these strange, fiery, fantastic energies, and created the splendour of substance and the love of it; created gold, and pearls, and crystal, and the sun that makes them gorgeous; and filled human fancy with all splendid thoughts; and given to the human touch its power of placing and brightening and perfecting, only that all these things may lead His creatures away from Him?   (1871)   235

Man is descended from some less highly organized form. The grounds upon which this conclusion rests will never be shaken, for the close similarity between man and the lower animals in embryonic development, as well as in innumerable points of structure and constitution ...are facts which cannot be disputed. They have long been known, but until recently they told us nothing with respect to the origin of man. Now, when viewed by the light of our knowledge of the whole organic world, their meaning is unmistakable. The great principle of evolution stands up clear and firm....It is incredible that all these facts should speak falsely. He who is not content to look, like a savage, at the phenomena of nature as disconnected, cannot any longer believe that man is the work of a separate act of creation. (1871)

286

On one occasion, when very young, I went for the week-end to the manor house of a squire and land-owner. On Sunday we went to church under charming circumstances. The squire's pew proved to be a square enclosure lined with green cloth, with a table in the centre and seats round the side. When we stood up, only a full-grown person could be seen over the top. In one corner was a fire-place and over it a small cupboard. As it was winter there was a fire in the fire-place and when the rector gave out his text the squire rose, poked the fire, opened the cupboard, took out a glass, and then a bottle of golden wine, poured out a glassful of the elixir, drank it, sat down again and went to sleep. To the boy it seemed that that man must be very happy who could sit in his own green pew, poke the fire during service, drink yellow wine and sleep in church, without being interfered with by a governess. Many fully grown persons may still share this childish view.

(*c.* 1880)

287

To be busy on Greek soil, under the light of the blue heaven, amid the scenes of ancient glory, in reading inscriptions, or putting together fragments of stone or marble, has a charm of another kind than that

which is to be found in the study of the language of ancient authors.
Yet even to appreciate truly the value of such remains, it is to the
higher study of the mind of Hellas and of her great men that we must
return, to finding some little pleasure by the way (like that of looking
at an autograph) in deciphering the handwriting of her children amid
the dust of her ruins.   (1881)

288

Consider for a moment the services rendered within quite recent years
by what has been called Prae-historic Archaeology, but which in truth
was never more Historic, in widening the horizon of our Past. It has
drawn aside the curtain and revealed the dawn. It has dispelled like
the unsubstantial phantoms of a dream, those preconceived notions as
to the origin of human arts and institutions at which Epicurus and
Lucretius already laughed, before the days of biblical chronology. It
has taught us that, at a time when Britain formed still a part of the
Continent of Europe with an arctic climate and another fauna; when
the Thames was flowing into the Rhine, and the Rhine itself, per-
chance, was a tributary of 'that ancient river', the river Solent; when
the very valley in which Oxford stands was only partly excavated,
Man was already in existence here fashioning his flint weapons to aid
him in his struggle against the sabre-toothed Tiger, or the woolly-
haired Rhinoceros. It has tracked him onwards to his cavern homes,
and dragged into the light his bone harpoons, and that flint scraper
wherewith he cleaned the shaggy hides for his apparel; it has unearthed
in the grottoes of Dordogne the earliest known relics of other than the
purest utilitarian art; it has followed him through the later periods of
the Age of Stone in Europe, whetting and polishing his tomahawks, or
delicately flaking out his arrow-heads and lance-heads. It has dived
to the lake bottoms, and reconstructed his pile-dwellings; it has fished
out the very clothes he wore, the spindle whorls that spun their threads,
the cereals that he had learnt to cultivate—nay, the very cakes he ate
and the caraway and poppy seeds wherewith he flavoured them. It
has shown us the beginnings of metallurgy...and has revealed to us
that at the close of the first Age of Metal, ancient lines of commerce
were already bringing the Mediterranean shores into direct connexion
with the Baltic lands of fur and amber.   (1884)

Nor must we overlook the probability of the constant inculcation in a belief in God on the minds of children producing so strong and perhaps an inherited effect on their brains not yet fully developed, that it would be as difficult for them to throw off their belief in God as for a monkey to throw off its instinctive fear and hatred of a snake.

(1886)

290

I propose to show in this book that a man's natural abilities are derived by inheritance, under exactly the same limitations as are the form and physical features of the whole organic world.   (1892)

291

Evangelical...that school of Protestants which maintains that the essence of 'the gospel' consists in the doctrine of salvation by faith in the atoning death of Christ and denies that either good works or the sacraments have any saving efficacy.   (1897)

292

There is no Wealth but Life. Life, including all its powers of love, of joy and of admiration. That country is the richest which nourishes the greatest number of noble and happy human beings; that man is richest who, having perfected the functions of his own life to the utmost, has also the widest helpful influence, both personal, and by means of his possessions, over the lives of others.

NOTES ON THE QUOTATIONS

1. C. C. F. Greville, *Journal of the reign of Queen Victoria, 1837–1852*, I (1885), 146. Greville, Clerk to the Council, was staying at Windsor on official business.

2. *Ibid.* I, 224.

3. G. Battiscombe, *Mrs. Gladstone* (1956), p. 40.

4. The Duke of Wellington on the ballot, cited by J. W. Dodds in *The Age of Paradox* (1953), p. 87.

5. Edward Walpole, cited by R. Nevill in *Life and Letters of Lady Dorothy Nevill* (1919), p. 19.

6. Samuel Smiles, *Autobiography* (1905), p. 104.

7. *Ibid.* p. 114.

8. Robert Lowe, cited by G. M. Young in *Early Victorian England* (1934), II, 380. The colony is Australia.

9. Robert Vaughan, *The Age of Great Cities* (1843), p. 143. Robert Vaughan, 1785–1868, was a Congregational Minister who in 1843 was Professor of History at University College, London.

10. John Ruskin, *Modern Painters*, I, pt. II, § 1, ch. 1.

11. Robert Vaughan, *The Age of Great Cities* (1843), p. 165. On Slangham Parish.

12. First Report of Constabulary Force Commissioners, pp. 70–2, quoted by R. Vaughan in *Age of Great Cities* (1843), p. 44. Braughing is now in Hertfordshire.

13. Friedrich Engels, *The Condition of the Working Classes in England in 1844* (1844).

14. *Ibid.*

15. Thomas Hughes, *Tom Brown at Oxford*, p. 435.

16. John Ruskin, Review of Lord Lindsay, *Sketches of the History of Christian Art*.

17. Thomas Carlyle, *Latter Day Pamphlets*, no. 2. John Howard, philanthropist, 1726(?)–90, was one of the first reformers of the shocking conditions in English prisons.

18. Thomas Carlyle, *Latter Day Pamphlets*, no. 3.

19. C. Hursthouse, *New Zealand* (1857), I, 164.

20. Thomas Carlyle, *Latter Day Pamphlets*, no. 1.

21. Thomas Carlyle, *Latter Day Pamphlets*, no. 4.

22. Thomas Carlyle, *Latter Day Pamphlets*, no. 3.

23. *The Year Book of Facts*, cited by C. Gibbs-Smith in *The Great Exhibition* (1950), p. 28.

24. Queen Victoria's Journal, cited by Y. ffrenche in *The Great Exhibition* (1950), p. 188.

25. The Prince Consort, at a Mansion House dinner on the Great Exhibition. Cited by Y. ffrenche in *The Great Exhibition* (1950), p. 51.

26. C. Tomlinson (ed.), *Cyclopedia of Useful Arts*. Cited by G. M. Young in *Early Victorian England* (1934), I, 220.

27. Herbert Spenser, *Essays* (1858 ed.), p. 109.

Notes

28. Marshal Canrobert, describing the state visit of Queen Victoria and the royal family to Saint-Cloud. Cited by E. E. P. Tisdall in *Queen Victoria's Private Life* (1961), p. 34.

29. Florence Nightingale, cited by Cecil Woodham Smith in *Florence Nightingale* (1950), p. 238.

30. John Ruskin, *Modern Painters*, II, pt. IV, ch. 16.

31. G. V. Cox, *Recollections of Oxford* (1868).

32. *The Life of Robert Owen, Written by Himself* (1857), p. xxii. Robert Owen, 1771–1858, wrote thus at the end of a long life of manufacturing and sociological activity.

33. *The Times*, 18 December 1858 ('Quakers' Changing Ways'). My mother has told me that nothing was more striking than the colours worn by emancipated Quaker ladies in her youth; grass green, magenta, Prussian blue, provided a consolation for generations of colour-starvation.

34. *The Times*, 5 August 1858.

35. *The Times*, 20 August 1859.

36. Quoted by Cecil Woodham Smith in *Florence Nightingale* (1950), p. 333. Florence Nightingale thus begins her *Notes on Hospitals*. It is of interest that she assumes that every patient should be assured of the entire care of at least one nurse.

37. *The Times*, 26 August 1861. Tests had just been held at Portsmouth to investigate the stopping power of armour plate.

38. *The Times*, 19 November 1861.

39. *The Times*, 2 June 1862.

40. *Charles Kingsley; His Letters and Memories* (1863), II, 148.

41. M. S. Watts, *George Frederick Watts* (1912), I. Said by G. F. Watts in his evidence before the Commission on the Royal Academy.

42. Mark Pattison, *Suggestions on Academical Organization* (1868), p. 316.

43. G. V. Cox, *Recollections of Oxford* (1868), p. 352.

44. Charles Dilke, *Greater Britain* (1869), p. 393. Sir Charles Dilke, Bt., 1843–1911, travelled round the world in 1868 before entering Parliament as a Radical.

45. *Ibid.* p. 354.

46. Francis Kilvert, *Diary*, ed. W. Plomer (1938), I, 93. (16 April 1870.)

47. John Ruskin, *Fors Clavigera* (*Works*, XXVII), p. 106. Written at the inn at Abingdon.

48. C. A. E. Moberly, *Dulce Domum* (1911), p. 230. George Moberly, Bishop of Salisbury, writing on 27 November 1871.

49. Francis Kilvert, *Diary*, ed. W. Plomer (1938), I, 334. (17 May 1871.)

50. *Ibid.* II, 199. (21 May 1872, Whitsun Tuesday.)

51. Charles Kingsley, *Town Geology* (1873). The book was primarily addressed to young clerks and skilled workmen. In 1873 the British North Borneo Chartered Company was founded to oust undesirable American adventurers from the country.

52. William Morris, cited by J. W. Mackail in *The Life of W. Morris* (1889), I, 302.

53. *Ibid.* p. 305.

54. Canon Barnett, cited by H. O. Barnett in *Canon Barnett* (1918), II, 270.

55. F. A. Barnett, Introduction to 2nd ed. of *Practicable Socialism. A Twenty Years' Retrospect* (1894), p. 3.

56. Canon Barnett, cited by H. O. Barnett in *Canon Barnett* (1918), II, 220.

57. Karl Baedeker, *London and its Environs: Handbook for Travellers*, 12th revised ed. (1900), p. 99.

58. *Ibid.* p. 99.

59. *Ibid.* p. 64.

60. *Ibid.* p. 1.

61. *Etiquette for the Ladies: Eighty Maxims on Dress, Manners and Accomplishments*, 4th ed. (1837). Cited by M. Lambert in *When Victoria began to Reign* (1937), p. 196.

62. Thomas Arnold writing to the Rev. Dr Hawkins, cited by A. P. Stanley in *Life of Dr. Arnold* (1839), I, 182.

63. *The Gentleman's Pocket Book of Etiquette* (by Arthur Freeling), cited by J. W. Dodds in *The Age of Paradox* (1953), p. 77.

64. Thomas Hughes, *Tom Brown at Oxford* (1861), p. 42. Hughes was writing of his own time at Oxford, in the years just before 1845.

65. *Ibid.* p. 20.

66. William Wayte Andrew, Vicar of Ketteringham, Norfolk, writing on 23 January 1841. Cited by O. Chadwick in *Victorian Miniature* (1960), p. 54.

67. *Ibid.* 15 June 1843.

68. Friedrich Engels, *The Condition of the Working Classes in England in 1844* (1844). Engels (1820–95), a German, was one of the founders of Collectivism.

69. A. Davidson, *Edward Lear* (1938), p. 17. Lear is writing from Lord Derby's house at Knowsley.

70. Friedrich Engels, *The Condition of the Working Classes in England in 1844* (1844).

71. Nathaniel Parker Willis, *Famous Persons and Famous Places* (1854), p. 187. He was writing of a visit to England in 1845.

72. Richard Monkton Milnes, cited by A. Fairfax Lucy in *Charlecote and the Lucys* (1958), p. 20.

73. S. Lambert, *The Railway King* (1934), pp. 177–8. The conversazione was at the Marquis of Northampton's house in Carlton House Terrace.

74. Samuel Smiles, *Autobiography* (1905), p. 155. Smiles was appearing before a select Committee of the House of Commons on the establishment of free public libraries.

75. Augustus J. C. Hare, *The Years with Mother*, ed. M. Barnes (1952), p. 60.

76. Alexis Soyer, *The Modern Housewife or Ménagère* (1849), pp. 150, 201, 286, 355, 361. The authoress is supposed to be the wife of a retired shopkeeper.

77. *Ibid.* p. 31.

78. *Ibid.* p. 401.

79. *Ibid.* p. 283. The dinner was supposed to be at 'city friends' of the writer's husband, at Balham Hill.

80. *Ibid.* p. 403.

81. Thomas Carlyle, *Latter Day Pamphlets*, no. 2.

82. Thomas Carlyle, *Latter Day Pamphlets*, no. 1.

83. J. H. Newman, *Idea of a University* (1852), Discourse VIII.

84. John Ruskin, *Stones of Venice*, II, ch. VI ('The Nature of Gothic'), xvi–xx.

85. Augustus J. C. Hare, *The Years with Mother*, ed. M. Barnes (1952), p. 92.

86. Lord Palmerston to the Commission on Purchase, cited by Cecil Woodham Smith in *The Reason Why*, Penguin ed. (1958), p. 30.

87. *Blair's First or Mother's Catechism*, 124th ed. (1856), p. 39.

88. *Ibid.* p. 39.

89. *The Times*, 18 January 1859.

90. G. V. Cox, *Recollections of Oxford* (1868), p. 428.

91. B. J. Armstrong, *A Norfolk Diary*, ed. H. B. J. Armstrong (1959), p. 65 (1 March 1859). The Rev. B. J. Armstrong was Vicar of East Dereham.

92. H. Mayhew, *London Labour and the London Poor*, i, 7.

93. *Ibid.* i, 20.

94. *Ibid.* i, 53.

95. *The Times*, 16 January 1863. Extract from a letter signed 'Z.A.'. The district would appear to be Gloucestershire.

96. E. Yates, *All the Year Round*, cited by G. M. Young in *Early Victorian England* (1934), ii, 311.

97. John Ruskin, *On the Present State of Modern Art* (*Works*, xix, 197).

98. Francis Kilvert, *Diary*, ed. W. Plomer (1938), iii, 144. (2 February 1875.)

99. M. R. Bobbitt, *With Dearest Love to All: Life and Letters of Lady Jebb* (1960), p. 109. From a letter written to her sister in the United States.

100. C. L. Eastlake, *Hints on Household Taste* (1878), p. 264.

101. M. R. Bobbitt, *With Dearest Love to All: Life and Letters of Lady Jebb* (1960), p. 162. Electric lighting had only been introduced in 1878.

102. Reprinted by courtesy of the Oxford University Press. The menu is intended for a hot summer evening, and is well chosen for its lightness and variety. It is so light, indeed, that no sorbet is served between the services.

103. W. Booth, *In Darkest England* (1890), p. 42.

104. *Ibid.* p. 25.

105. *Ibid.* p. 25.

106. *The Times*, 10 October 1961.

107. *Wot Cher! Or, Knocked 'em in the Old Kent Road.* One of Albert Chevalier's Cockney songs, sung by him to music by his brother (Charles Ingle).

108. Mrs C. S. Peel, *10/- a Head for House Books*, pp. xii, 4, 47, 133.

109. Gabriel Tschumi, *Royal Chef* (1954), p. 32.

110. Lady Diana Cooper, *The Rainbow Comes and Goes* (1958), pp. 34–5.

111. Karl Baedeker, *London and its Environs: Handbook for Travellers*, 12th revised ed. (1900), p. 332.

112. *Sunday Times*, 10 July 1900.

113. Emily Eden, *Semi-Attached Couple*. Written *c.* 1830, published 1860.

114. Mrs John Sandford, *Woman in her Social and Domestic Character* (?1837).

115. R. E. Leader, *Life of John Arthur Roebuck* (1897), p. 117. Written from Glasgow.

116. Charlotte Brontë writing to her sister Emily, cited by Mrs Gaskell in *Life of Charlotte Brontë*.

117. Alfred Lord Tennyson, *The Princess*.

118. *Quarterly Review* on *Jane Eyre*, cited by J. W. Dodds in *Age of Paradox* (1953), p. 311.

119. Florence Nightingale's diary of her life at home, cited by Cecil Woodham Smith in *Florence Nightingale* (1950), p. 92. Florence Nightingale was writing shortly before her thirty-second birthday.

120. Florence Nightingale in a letter, cited by Cecil Woodham Smith in *Florence Nightingale* (1950), p. 118.

121. Charles Kingsley, *Glaucus, or the Wonders of the Shore* (1855), p. 4.

122. Florence Nightingale, *Notes on Nursing* (1860), p. 76.

123. *Ibid.* p. 73.

124. Mrs Beeton, *Household Management*, preface.

125. *The Times*, 21 January 1862. Extract from a letter signed 'Common Sense'.

126. Richard Whately, D.D., *Miscellaneous Remains* (1864).

127. Florence Nightingale to John Stuart Mill, who asked her to be a member of the first Committee of the London National Society for Women's Suffrage. She refused. Cited by Cecil Woodham Smith in *Florence Nightingale* (1950), p. 487.

128. C. M. Yonge in a letter to Emily Davies about women's colleges. Cited by G. Battiscombe in *Charlotte Mary Yonge* (1943), p. 146.

129. C. M. Yonge, *Womankind* (c. 1870). In fact, Charlotte Yonge was noticeably plain.

130. J. H. Ewing, *A Flat Iron for a Farthing* (1873).

131. *Daily Telegraph*, 18 March 1873. Quoted by Ruskin in *Fors Clavigera*, May (*Works*, XXVII, 536).

132. Some of Miss Nightingale's comments on the nurses who came to see her from the Nightingale Training School at St Thomas's. Those called 'Miss' were 'ladies' of more genteel education, intended for administrative posts. Cited by L. Seymer, *Florence Nightingale's Nurses; the Nightingale Training School. 1860–1960* (1960), p. 697.

133. C. L. Eastlake, *Hints on Household Taste*, 4th ed. (1878), p. 8.

134. Augustus J. C. Hare, *The Years with Mother*, ed. M. Barnes (1952), p. 27.

135. Thomas Arnold writing to the Rev. G. Cornish. Cited by A. P. Stanley in *Life of Dr. Arnold*, I, 161.

136. Thomas Arnold, *Miscellaneous Works* (1845), p. 226. Cited by T. W. Bamford in *Thomas Arnold* (1960), p. 176.

137. *Athenaeum*, 22 April 1843, p. 392. The Martyrs' Memorial had just been completed, and was universally admired; while the Taylorian Building, also just finished, continued the classical tradition.

138. Diary of the Rev. A. B. Evans, cited by Joan Evans in *Time and Chance* (1943), p. 56. The Royal Agricultural Society, of which the aim was to educate the farmer, first met in 1839.

139. Thomas Carlyle, *Latter Day Pamphlets*, no. 3. A new competitive basis for the upper ranks of the Civil Service had been proposed.

140. A. K. Boyd, *History of Radley College* (1948), p. 40. No sweets or fruit were provided and no tuckboxes or supplies from home were allowed—but beer was provided at meals, two glasses at dinner.

141. Second Report of the Commissioners on the Great Exhibition, cited by Y. ffrenche in *The Great Exhibition*, p. 283.

142. J. H. Newman, *Idea of a University* (1852), preface.

143. *Ibid.* Discourse, VI.

144. W. A. Fearon, *The Passing of Old Winchester*, p. 20.

145. F. D. Maurice, *Learning and Working* (1854).

146. From Pusey's tract on 'Collegiate and Professorial Teaching and Discipline', cited by H. P. Liddon in *Life of Edward Bouverie Pusey* (1898), III, 390.

147. Herbert Spencer, *Education* (1861), p. 170.

148. *The Times*, 23 November 1861. The promoter of the scheme was the Rev. N. Woodard, founder of the various Woodard schools. The Vice-Chancellor was in the Chair at the meeting, and the speakers included Mr Gladstone, Chancellor of the Exchequer.

149. Benjamin Jowett writing to Sidney Irwin, a schoolboy at Wellington. Cited by G. Faber in *Jowett: a Portrait with Background* (1957), p. 63.

150. *The Times*, 2 September 1861.

151. John Ruskin, *Unto this Last*, preface (*Works*, XVI, 21).

152. Mark Pattison, *Suggestions on Academical Organization* (1868), p. 126.

153. *Ibid.* p. 62.

154. *Ibid.* p. 241.

155. F. Galton, *Hereditary Genius* (1892 ed.), p. 12.

156. *Ibid.* p. 21.

157. Charles Kingsley, *Town Geology* (1873), p. xv.

158. *Ibid.* p. xxxiii.

159. *Ibid.* p. xi.

160. G. Faber, *Jowett: A Portrait with Background* (1957), p. 81. Tuckwell is writing about Jowett, with whom he had been walking on Exmoor.

161. M. C. F. Morris, *Yorkshire Reminiscences* (1922), p. 126.

162. Quoted by H. O. Barnett in *Canon Barnett* (1918), I, 327.

163. *Ibid.* p. 288. Dame Henrietta Barnett describes a district school at Forest Gate, for children chargeable to the Workhouse Unions of Whitechapel and Poplar.

164. John Ruskin, *Praeterita* (*Works*, XXXV, 30).

165. Charlotte Brontë writing to Mrs Gaskell. Cited by Mrs Gaskell in *Life of Charlotte Brontë*.

166. A. Davidson, *Edward Lear* (1938), p. 6.

167. Samuel Smiles, *Autobiography* (1905), p. 82.

168. Thomas Arnold writing to Sir T. S. Pasley. Cited by A. P. Stanley in *Life of Dr Arnold* (1839), I, 158.

169. H. Pengelly, *A Memoir of William Pengelly* (1897), p. 13.

170. Quoted by R. S. Lambert, *The Railway King* (1934), p. 127.

171. Augustus J. C. Hare, *The Years with Mother*, ed. M. Barnes (1952), p. 42.

172. H. J. Fuller and V. Hammersley, *Thackeray's Daughter* (1951).

173. E. B. Ellman, *Recollections of a Sussex Parson* (1912), p. 141.

174. Augustus J. C. Hare, *The Years with Mother*, ed. M. Barnes (1952), p. 54.

175. *Ibid.* p. 67.

176. E. B. Ellman, *Recollections of a Sussex Parson* (1912), p. 147.

177. C. H. Pearson, *Memorials*, cited by L. James in *A Forgotten Genius, Sewell* (1945), p. 37.

178. N. Barlow (ed.), *Autobiography of Charles Darwin* (1958), p. 108.

179. C. C. F. Greville, *A Journal of the Reign of Queen Victoria, 1837–1852*, pt. II, vol. 3, p. 402.

180. John Ruskin, *Works*, X, xxvi. Quoting C. Eliot Norton.

181. From a letter from Mrs Gaskell to Catherine Winkworth, 20 October 1854. Cited by Cecil Woodham Smith in *Florence Nightingale* (1950), p. 127.

182. H. J. Fuller and V. Hammersley, *Thackeray's Daughter* (1951), p. 86.

183. C. A. E. Moberly (on her mother, wife of the Head Master of Winchester), *Dulce Domum* (1911), p. 155.

184. B. J. Armstrong (Vicar of East Dereham), *A Norfolk Diary*. ed. H. B. J. Armstrong (1949).

185. Francis Kilvert, *Diary*, ed. W. Plomer (1938), I, 75 (5 April 1870).

186. E. T. Cook, preface to Ruskin's *Works*, XX, xxiii. The description is of Ruskin.

187. M. A. Bayfield and J. D. Duff, *Collected Literary Essays by A. W. Verrall*. Cited by C. Hassall in *Edward Marsh* (1959), p. 41. The description is of Verrall's lecturing technique.

188. J. R. Green, *Oxford Studies* (1901), cited by C. Day Lewis and C. Tenby in *Anatomy of Oxford* (1938), p. 111.

189. John Ruskin, 'The Poetry of Architecture', *Architectural Magazine* (1837–8).

190. *Athenaeum*, 26 June 1840, p. 493.

191. Friedrich Engels, *The Condition of the Working Classes in England in 1844* (1844).

192. *Ibid.*

193. *Athenaeum*, 22 June 1844. An advertisement on the title-page.

194. H. J. Fuller and V. Hammersley, *Thackeray's Daughter* (1851), p. 60.

195. John Ruskin, *The Seven Lamps of Architecture*, ch. IV, § 19, 300.

196. *Reports of Juries*, II, 1602 (1851).

197. *Ibid.* II, 1588 ff., 'Supplementary Report on design', by R. Redgrave, R.A.

198. *Illustrated London News*, 4 October 1851, cited by A. Bøe in *From Gothic Revival to Functional Form* (Oslo, 1957), p. 11.

199. C. A. E. Moberly, *Dulce Domum* (1911), p. 99. Emily Moberly was going with her family for a holiday at Fieldhouse Farm.

200. John Ruskin, *Edinburgh Lectures*, I.

201. Mrs Gaskell, *Life of Charlotte Brontë* (1857). The town is Keighley, Yorkshire.

202. Florence Nightingale, *Notes on Nursing* (1860), p. 10.

203. *The Times*, 24 April 1861.

204. *Charles Kingsley: His Letters and Memories of his Life* (1877), II, 175.

205. R. Kerr, *The Gentleman's House* (1864), p. 143.

206. *Ibid.* p. 249.

207. *Ibid.* p. 167. It was in this year that Florence Nightingale, to the astonishment of her committee, had her home for governesses at 1, Harley Street, equipped with piped hot water on every floor and 'a windlass' for bringing up and taking down trays.

Notes

208. Anon. *A Plea for Art in the Home* (before 1879), p. 39.

209. *Macmillan's Magazine*, September 1871, cited by G. M. Trevelyan in *English Social History* (1944), p. 571.

210. C. L. Eastlake, *Hints on Household Taste*, 4th ed. (1878), p. 136.

211. J. H. Ewing, *A Flat Iron for a Farthing* (1873).

212. Max Beerbohm, '1880', *The Yellow Book*, IV (January 1895), p. 275

213. Mrs Haweis, *Art of Decoration* (1881), p. 10.

214. William Booth, *In Darkest London* (1890), p. 70. On the life of a tramp.

215. H. Nicolson, *King George V* (1952), p. 51. York Cottage became the residence of the Duke and Duchess of York on their marriage.

216. C. C. F. Greville, *Journal of the Reign of Queen Victoria, 1837–1852* (1885), I, p. 11.

217. A. R. Wallace, *The Wonderful Century* (1898), p. 4.

218. Samuel Smiles, *Lives of the Engineers* (1862), III, 345.

219. Samuel Smiles, *Industrial Biography: Iron Workers and Tool Makers* (1863), p. 290.

220. Friedrich Engels, *Condition of the Working Classes in England in 1844* (1844).

221. Thorold Rogers, *Cobden and Political Opinions* (1841), p. 20.

222. Samuel Smiles, *Lives of the Engineers* (1862), III, 365.

223. Samuel Smiles, *Autobiography* (1905), p. 95. On a great Suffrage Festival held at the mill, 21 January 1841.

224. Friedrich Engels, *The Condition of the Working Classes in England in 1844* (1844).

225. *Ibid.*

226. *Ibid.*

227. *Ibid.* introduction.

228. Lord Macaulay, *Works*, VIII (1846), p. 360. From a speech.

229. Samuel Smiles, *Lives of the Engineers* (1862), III, p. 380.

230. *The Standard*, 19 December, cited by R. S. Lambert in *The Railway King* (1934), p. 198.

231. Harriet Evans writing to Sebastian Dickinson in India. Cited by Joan Evans in *Time and Chance* (1943), p. 74.

232. R. S. Lambert, *The Railway King* (1934), p. 250 (quoting *The Times*).

233. R. S. Lambert, *The Railway King* (1934), p. 250. An eye-witness of Hudson's appearance before the Committee of Inquiry, 14 April 1849, is cited.

234. *The Yorkshireman*, February 1849, cited by R. S. Lambert in *The Railway King* (1934), p. 250.

235. From the farewell address of the Secretary of the Flint Glass Makers. Cited by B. and S. Webb, *History of Trade Unionism* (1920), p. 201. n. 2. Most of the larger Unions established an Emigration Fund, but they were not big enough to diminish available labour appreciably, and it was found that the feckless emigrated and came home again at the Society's expense.

236. H. Spencer, *Railway Morals and Railway Policy* (1855), p. 4.

237. B. J. Armstrong, *A Norfolk Diary*, ed. H. B. J. Armstrong (1949), p. 36.

238. *Blair's First or Mother's Catechism*, 124th ed. (1856).

239. Samuel Smiles, *Self Help* (1859), XI.

240. John Ruskin, *The Two Paths* (1859), XVI, 336.

241. *The Times*, 11 July 1860.

242. Francis Kilvert, *Diary*, ed. W. Plomer (1938), II, 102.

243. Letter to Ruskin from a working woman, quoted in *Fors Clavigera*, XXVIII, 65.

244. John Ruskin, *Fors Clavigera* (1877), August, XXIX, 173.

245. William Morris, 'Making the Best of It' (*Collected Works*, XXII, 114). Quoted by N. Pevsner in *Mathew Digby Wyatt* (1950), p. 28.

246. *The Times*, 8 May 1881.

247. Karl Baedeker, *London and its Environs: Handbook for Travellers*, 12th revised ed. (1900), p. 32.

248. Arnold writing to W. W. Hull, cited by A. P. Stanley, *Life of Dr. Arnold*, I, 32. In 1838 Arnold was alone in voting in the Senate against the admission of Jews to the University of London. In 1847 the first Jew was elected to Parliament when Rothschild came in as member for the City of London.

249. *Charles Kingsley; His Letters and Memories of his Life* (1877), I, 38.

250. John Ruskin, *Praeterita* (*Works*, ed. Cook and Wedderburn, XXXV, 132).

251. Arnold writing to H. Fox, who intended to be a missionary. Cited by A. P. Stanley in *Life of Dr. Arnold* (1840), I, 201.

252. The Rev. J. H. Newman to Pusey, cited by H. P. Liddon in *The Life of Edward Bouverie Pusey* (1893), I, 135.

253. Thomas Hughes, *Tom Brown at Oxford* (1861), p. 113. By 1865 Jowett said that muscular Christianity 'is gone out' and that Anglo-Catholicism had become aesthetic (Mackail, I, 146).

254. Thomas Hughes, *Tom Brown at Oxford* (1861), p. 86.

255. *Ibid.* p. 8. Pea-coats, more usually pea-jackets, were the duffel-coats of early Victorian young men, and were likewise of naval origin.

256. By Thomas Binney (1798–1874), Congregational minister and liturgical reformer.

257. Hugh Miller, *Footprints of the Creator: or The Asterolepts of Stromness*, 3rd ed. (1850), p. 14.

258. A. W. Pugin, *Contrasts*, 2nd ed. (1841), p. 49.

259. R. Vaughan, *The Age of Great Cities* (1843), p. 305.

260. Mark Pattison, *Memoirs* (1885), p. 236.

261. *Athenaeum*, 11 October 1845, p. 995.

262. Quoted by H. P. Liddon, *Life of Edward Bouverie Pusey* (1898), III, 171.

263. Jowett writing to a friend, cited by G. Faber in *Jowett: Portrait with Background* (1957), p. 214.

264. Advertisement in *Athenaeum*, 18 November 1848, p. 1138.

265. Augustus J. C. Hare, *The Years with Mother*, ed. M. Barnes (1952), p. 55.

266. B. J. Armstrong, *A Norfolk Diary*, ed. H. B. J. Armstrong (1949), p. 13.

267. Pusey writing to A. P. Stanley, cited by V. H. H. Green in *Oxford Common Room* (1957), p. 181.

268. R. Chenevix Trench, D.D., Dean of Westminster, *On the Study of Words* (1851).

Notes

269. J. H. Newman, *Idea of a University* (1852), preface.

270. Anny Thackeray (aged 15) writing to her father, cited by H. J. Fuller and V. Hammersley in *Thackeray's Daughter* (1951), p. 72.

271. Macmillans' list (1855).

272. John Evans writing to his fiancée, after he had verified Boucher de Perthes's publication of the evidence for the existence of palaeolithic man. Cited by Joan Evans in *Time and Chance*, p. 100.

273. T. H. Huxley, after the death of his son, writing to Charles Kingsley.

274. Florence Nightingale, *Notes on Nursing* (1860), p. 5.

275. *The Times*, 1 July 1861. *Essays and Reviews*, the famous collaborative volume in which a number of theologians expounded their critical interpretations of the Scriptures, had been censured by the Convocation of Canterbury.

276. T. H. Huxley writing to Charles Kingsley, cited by C. Bibby in *T. H. Huxley* (1958), p. 61.

277. T. H. Huxley, *Man's Place in Nature* (1863), p. 108.

278. *Ibid.* p. 103.

279. *Letters of General C. G. Gordon to his Sister* (1888), p. 12.

280. *Ibid.* p. 36.

281. F. Galton, *Hereditary Genius*, 1892 ed., p. 189.

282. Charles Darwin, *The Descent of Man*, 1922 ed., p. 3.

283. Sir William Thomson (Lord Kelvin), Presidential Address to the Royal Society, 1871.

284. John Ruskin, *Notes on Turin Gallery* (*Works*, ed. Cook and Wedderburn, v. p. xii).

285. Charles Darwin, *The Descent of Man*, 1922 ed., p. 926.

286. Arthur J. Ashton, K.C., *As I went on my way* (1924), p. 3.

287. G. Faber, *Jowett: A Portrait with Background* (1957), p. 391. Jowett, who had never been to Greece, wrote as a typical classical scholar.

288. Arthur Evans, in his Inaugural Lecture as Keeper of the Ashmolean. Cited by Joan Evans in *Time and Chance* (1943), p. 270.

289. Charles Darwin, *Autobiography*, ed. N. Barlow (1958).

290. F. Galton, *Hereditary Genius*, 1892 ed., introductory chapter, p. 1.

291. *New English Dictionary* (1897), III, 329.

292. John Ruskin, *Unto this Last* (*Works*, XVII, 105).

LIST OF ILLUSTRATIONS

Frontispiece. Victoria, aged 35, from a painting by Winterhalter
Radio Times Hulton Picture Library

1 Queen Victoria and Prince Albert in Scotland, by Sir Edwin Landseer   *page* 1
Radio Times Hulton Picture Library

2 A portrait drawing of Queen Victoria, dated 19 August 1838   11
G. A. Parrett, Esq.

3 Queen Victoria's private sitting-room, Osborne House, Isle of Wight   12
Crown copyright

4 Queen Victoria and Prince Albert: a photograph   13
Victoria and Albert Museum

5 An informal picture of Queen Victoria at Abergeldie in 1889, taken by   14
the Princess of Wales, later Queen Alexandra
Gernsheim Collection

6 Silver-gilt table-centre designed by Prince Albert with representations   20
of four of the Queen's dogs, executed by Robert Garrard, 1842
Crown copyright

7 The Crystal Palace   20
Victoria and Albert Museum

8 Queen Victoria opening the Great Exhibition at the Crystal Palace,   21
May 1851, by H. Selous
Radio Times Hulton Picture Library

9 The funeral procession of Prince Albert   22
Illustrated London News

10 The Albert Memorial in Hyde Park, designed by Sir Gilbert Scott and   23
completed in 1872
C. Handley-Read, Esq.

11 The House of Commons, 1860, from a painting by John Phillip   28
Lt.-Col. W. M. E. Denison

12 Members of Parliament passing the Tellers, *c.* 1870   29
Radio Times Hulton Picture Library

13 The Grand Staircase of the Foreign Office, London, designed by   30
Sir Gilbert Scott, *c.* 1865
Country Life

14 Bottleneck in Park Lane between Brick Street and Piccadilly, 1863   31
Copyright Reginald Colby, Esq.

15 Carriages entering and leaving Hyde Park in 1872, from a drawing by   32
Gustave Doré
Radio Times Hulton Picture Library

List of
Illustrations

16 'On the Dogger Bank', by W. C. Stanfield, 1846 *page* 34
  Victoria and Albert Museum

17 'The Long Engagement', by Alfred Hughes, 1859 35
  Birmingham City Art Gallery

18 The cover from Moore's *Irish Melodies* 36

19 From a drawing by George du Maurier, 1880 47

20 Fox-hunting: 'The Pleasures of Hope' 50
  Radio Times Hulton Picture Library

21 'The Road to Ruin—Ascot', by W. P. Frith 51
  Private Collection, Turin

22 'The entrance of the stewards and orphans at the dinner of the Indigent 55
  Orphans' Friends' Benevolent Institution', from an etching by George
  Cruikshank, 1836

23 'Coffee stall, early morning', by Gustave Doré 56
  Radio Times Hulton Picture Library

24 'Wentworth Street, Whitechapel', by Gustave Doré, *c.* 1870 57
  Radio Times Hulton Picture Library

25 Detail from 'Work', by Ford Madox Brown, 1863 58
  Birmingham City Art Gallery

26 Detail from 'Valleys thick with Corn', by R. Redgrave, 1865 59
  Birmingham City Art Gallery

27 'Temptation: A Fruit Stall', by S. Smith, 1850 60
  Victoria and Albert Museum

28 'Going to Table', from a drawing by George du Maurier 68

29 'The children of Elhanan Bicknell', by S. P. Denning, 1841 70
  Victoria and Albert Museum

30 Daguerreotype of a gentleman, *c.* 1845 71
  Gernsheim Collection

31 'Ramsgate Sands', by W. P. Frith 72
  Radio Times Hulton Picture Library

32 'Bedtime', by Arthur Hughes 74

33 'Children by a pond at Fulham', by C. Hunt, 1859 84
  Mrs Mollem Burt

34 Harvest-Home, 1843. The annual feast for tenants and farm-workers in 85
  the Squire's barn
  Radio Times Hulton Picture Library

35 Michaelmas Goose Fair, 1873 85
  Radio Times Hulton Picture Library

250

36 The first English touring cricket team on their way to America, 1859 *page* 86
    Radio Times Hulton Picture Library

37 Hyde Park in the Season, 1870   87
    Radio Times Hulton Picture Library

38 Eton and Harrow Match, 1880, from a drawing by George du Maurier   87

39 'The Music Lesson', a photograph of about 1857   88

40 'Blue Gate Fields, London', by Gustave Doré   95
    Radio Times Hulton Picture Library

41 'Whip-behind', from *Guttersnipes* by Phil May, 1896   96

42 From a drawing by George du Maurier, 1880   103

43 'Garden Flowers', by W. P. Frith   105
    Birmingham City Art Gallery

44 Adeline, Countess of Cardigan, *c.* 1845, by R. Buckner   106
    The Marquess of Ailesbury

45 'The Travelling Companions', by Augustus Egg, 1862   107
    Birmingham City Art Gallery

46 'The Widow's Mite', by J. E. Millais   109
    Birmingham City Art Gallery

47 A window fernery and fountain   113
    Radio Times Hulton Picture Library

48 Family photograph: Mother and the girls, *c.* 1865   114

49 A game of tennis. Flowing clothes held in by embroidered aprons. By 115
    George du Maurier, 1880

50 The first women students to be admitted to the University of   116
    Cambridge, photographed at Hitchin, 1869
    Girton College, Cambridge

51 Harrow School Room, a drawing by T. W. Pugin   121
    Radio Times Hulton Picture Library

52 A school run on the monitorial system, 1839   124
    Radio Times Hulton Picture Library

53 Dinner-time at the Clare-market Ragged School   124
    Radio Times Hulton Picture Library

54 Eton College, the Upper Grammar School, 1861   125
    Radio Times Hulton Picture Library

55 Photograph of a village school, *c.* 1856   126
    Radio Times Hulton Picture Library

56 Rugby School from the Close, *c.* 1870   131
    Radio Times Hulton Picture Library

List of
Illustrations

57 St Andrew's College and Industrial Schools, Chardstock,   *page* 132
    Dorset, 1861
    Radio Times Hulton Picture Library

58 A group of Eton boys, *c.* 1890   133
    Radio Times Hulton Picture Library

59 Undergraduates at Cambridge, *c.* 1900   134
    Radio Times Hulton Picture Library

60 'Feeding the Cat.' A photograph by O. G. Rejlander, *c.* 1857   147
    Gernsheim Collection

61 Elizabeth Browning, by Field Talfourd, 1859   148
    National Portrait Gallery

62 John Ruskin, by George Richmond   149
    National Portrait Gallery

63 Charles Kingsley, by Lowes Dickinson, 1862   150
    National Portrait Gallery

64 William Morris, by G. F. Watts   151
    National Portrait Gallery

65 W. E. Gladstone, by Phil May, 1893   152

66 Scarisbrick Hall, Lancashire. The south front with Pugin's Great Hall   160
    in the centre
    Country Life

67 'Orchard' tapestry, designed by William Morris, 1890   162
    Victoria and Albert Museum

68 'Over London by Rail', by Gustave Doré   165
    Radio Times Hulton Picture Library

69 Elevation and plan for a small house in the Tudor style   166
    R.I.B.A. Library

70 Exhibits at the Great Exhibition in the Crystal Palace, from the *Art* 169
    Journal Illustrated Catalogue, 1851

71 The Saloon at Highclere Castle, decorated by Thomas Allom, *c.* 1862   170
    Country Life

72 'Allanbank', a house in Camden Road, London, designed by   171
    Henry Hodge, 1863
    National Buildings Record

73 The entrance front at Waddesdon Manor, Buckinghamshire. The house   172
    was designed for Baron Ferdinand de Rothschild by G. H. Destailleur
    in 1874
    Country Life

74 Bronze ornament, by San Giovanni, exhibited at the Great Exhibition,   174
    from the *Art Journal Illustrated Catalogue*, 1851

75 'Renaissance' sideboard exhibited by T. W. Caldecott at the Great   *page* 174
Exhibition, from the *Art Journal Illustrated Catalogue*, 1851

76 Bedford Park, London. A group of houses in a middle-class residential   180
area, *c.* 1880
National Buildings Record

77 Mabel Love's drawing-room, *c.* 1890   181
Radio Times Hulton Picture Library

78 Lily Langtry's bedroom, *c.* 1896   181
Radio Times Hulton Picture Library

79 The Port of London, 1842   184
Radio Times Hulton Picture Library

80 Leeds from Holbeck Junction, 1868   186
Radio Times Hulton Picture Library

81 Women engaged in power-loom weaving, from an engraving by   190
Thomas Allom, *c.* 1840
Radio Times Hulton Picture Library

82 New hydraulic lift at the Victoria Docks, London, 1858   191
Radio Times Hulton Picture Library

83 General view of the new docks at Millwall, London, 1868   192
Radio Times Hulton Picture Library

84 Unloading tea-ships in the East India Docks, London, 1867   194
Radio Times Hulton Picture Library

85 The London–Chatham–Dover Railway experimented with the issuing of   199
cheap workmen's tickets, *c.* 1865
Radio Times Hulton Picture Library

86 New saloon carriage on the London, Brighton and South Coast Railway,   199
1873
Radio Times Hulton Picture Library

87 An express train on the London to Brighton line, 1875   200
Radio Times Hulton Picture Library

88 Handling merchandise at London docks, 1880   201
Radio Times Hulton Picture Library

89 The industrial aspect of Leeds from Richmond Hill, 1885   206
Radio Times Hulton Picture Library

90 'The Scapegoat', by W. Holman Hunt   208
The Trustees of the Lady Lever Art Gallery

91 'Christ in the Carpenter's Shop', by J. E. Millais   213
Radio Times Hulton Picture Library

92 The Oxford Museum, from a photograph of 1858   214
Radio Times Hulton Picture Library

93 The Anglican Cathedral, Truro, Cornwall   215
Radio Times Hulton Picture Library

94   Professor T. H. Huxley, from a photograph, *c.* 1890   *page* 216
      Radio Times Hulton Picture Library

95   Cardinal Newman, from a photograph by H. Barraud, 1887   217
      Gernsheim Collection

96   Charles Darwin, by Marian Collier, 1878   218
      National Portrait Gallery

97   Keble College, Oxford   225
      Radio Times Hulton Picture Library

98   Wesleyan Chapel, Blackpool, Lancashire   225
      Radio Times Hulton Picture Library

99   Sunday observance, *c.* 1900   226
      Radio Times Hulton Picture Library

100   The Altar, Brompton Oratory, London   227
      Radio Times Hulton Picture Library

101   The British Museum, Natural History, South Kensington, London, 1873–80   233
      Radio Times Hulton Picture Library

102   The British Museum, London   234
      Radio Times Hulton Picture Library

ACKNOWLEDGEMENTS

Permission to use quotations and photographs is gratefully acknowledged to owners of the copyrights as follows:

Quotations. Nos. 3, 119, 120, 127, 128, 181, 214 (Messrs Constable & Co. Ltd); nos. 46, 49, 50, 98, 185, 242 (Messrs Jonathan Cape Ltd); nos. 48, 54, 56, 69, 162, 163, 166, 183, 189 (Messrs John Murray Ltd); nos. 73, 75, 85, 134, 174, 265 (Messrs George Allen & Unwin Ltd); nos. 99, 101, 149, 160, 287 (Messrs Faber & Faber Ltd); no. 109 (Messrs William Kimber & Co. Ltd); no. 110 (Messrs Rupert Hart-Davies Ltd); no. 132 (The Pitman Medical Publishing Co. Ltd); no. 161 (Oxford University Press); nos. 172, 182, 194, 270 (Messrs W. J. Pollock & Co. Ltd); nos. 173, 176 (Messrs Skeffington & Sons Ltd); nos. 177, 234 (Messrs Longmans, Green & Co. Ltd); no. 267 (Messrs Edward Arnold (Publishers) Ltd); no. 276 (Messrs C. A. Watts & Co. Ltd); no. 286 (Messrs Nisbet & Co. Ltd).

Photographs. Grateful acknowledgement to all copyright holders shown in the List of Illustrations on pp. 249–54.

DATE DUE

FE 18 '67			
DE 8 '69			
DE 19 '69			
SE 9 '70			
NO 1 '70			
FE 4 '75			
OC 10 '78			
DE 19 '78			
MY 27 '80			
MY 15 '82			
MY 3 '84			
AP 14 '87			
SE 12 '89			
AP 17 '90			
SE 01 '92			
NO 4 '93			
GAYLORD			PRINTED IN U.S.A.